Home Field
Advantage

Todd

God Bless
Press On

Coach McCoy

Published by:
Flippen Group
1199 Haywood Dr.
College Station, Texas 77845
www.flippengroup.com

Printed in the United States of America

Library of Congress Cataloging-in-Publication Data

McCoy, Brad
home field advantage : a playbook on life, leadership and legacy / brad mccoy

ISBN-10: 0983587108
EAN-13: 9780983587101

Bringing out the best in people

Home Field Advantage

A Playbook on Life, Leadership and Legacy

Brad McCoy

About the Author

Brad McCoy
Athletic Director of Flippen Sports

Brad McCoy joined the Flippen Group after twenty-seven years as a coach and teacher in the public school system. During this time, he gained extensive knowledge about factors that determine the success of athletic programs and developed a passion for growing athletes into great leaders.

Brad graduated from Abilene Christian University, where he played football from 1979 to 1983. He has served as an athletic director, head football coach and teacher during his career in education. His impressive overall record, along with four State Championship appearances and two state titles, speak for the success of his teams. Despite his notable accomplishments in sports, he is most driven by the personal success of his athletes stating, "I want our guys to grow up and develop into fine players on the field, but more importantly, I want them to turn into great husbands, dads, business leaders, church leaders and men that make this world a better place."

Brad employs this philosophy in his personal life as much as his professional life. He and Debra, his wife of 26 years, have raised three sons who are all high performers, both on and off the field. His oldest son, Colt, played for the University of Texas and set national records for most wins ever by a quarterback and highest completion percentage ever by a quarterback along with 47 other national, Big 12 and school records. He is currently the starting quarterback for the Cleveland Browns. Chance, a receiver at Hardin-Simmons University, was a three-time All State receiver in high school and played for state championships in football, basketball and track. Case lead his high school team to the state championship and was named to multiple All State teams. He graduated with honors and enrolled at the University of Texas to follow in his brother's footsteps as quarterback for the Longhorns.

Serving as a Teen Leadership teacher and consultant, Brad has been involved with the Flippen Group for over 15 years. In 2010, Brad came on full time as Athletic Director of Flippen Sports. He and Debra reside in Graham, Texas.

Preface
Brad McCoy

The goal of a leader is simple—others' success. That has been my goal with my family as well. The question is always the same, "How can I be better as a dad and a husband?" For those who know me, you know that I am a work in progress. For those of you who have heard of our family either through our sons or the media, I want you to know that my greatest goal is to make my life count and I think the best way to do that is as a great father and husband. I'm also thankful for forgiveness and the many opportunities that Debra has given me over the years to practice asking.

Our family is much like all others, we have our challenges and successes but we never stray from our commitment to, and love for each other. I think the one thing that determines whether a person has a good family life is their ability to admit when they are wrong and to turn loose of things when they need to be let go. Growing is not for the faint of heart.

There is a verse in Proverbs that we have tried to live by, *"Train up a child in the way he should go and when he is old he will not stray from it"*.

What an amazing promise—I am now the father of grown men 25, 23 and 19 years old. Debra and I still pray daily for the priorities in their lives and the decisions they make, and that they always put God first in everything they do. We don't have the daily interaction we always had with our kids and aren't responsible for their everyday care and decision-making. We hope that we have done a respectable job of "preparing the child for the path, and not the path for the child".

As parents we understand (but don't necessarily like it) that our role has changed and become that of a "consultant".

So, from one set of parents to another, I hope you enjoy the stories and journey of a man who wants to be better because of a greater love that lives within him.

That's the goal of the *Home Field Advantage*—to show that it's the commitment to your "home team" that produces winners—on and off the field.

Special Thanks

As I think of the people that have meant the most to me throughout the years, there is no way to mention all who have contributed to the growth of my family and career. However, there is no way any of this would have happened if not for the love, leadership, and dedication from my parents, Burl and Jan McCoy. Their teaching and discipline are the foundation of my ability to be a good father and coach. They are the greatest influence in my life and the greatest parents and grandparents that anyone could hope to have. I love them both with all my heart.

Debra is the love of my life and the best wife, mom, and coach's wife in the world. She has stuck by me through tough times both on and off the field. She is the glue that holds our family together and also sacrificed all she has for her boys and me. My boys, Case, Chance, and Colt have been the highlight of my life. I cannot begin to tell you how proud I am for the men they have become. I thank them for allowing me to share their lives with others who might benefit from our struggles and successes.

We have such a great family support system from my parents and Debra's parents, the late Bill and Sarah Woodruff, my brother and sister, Michael and Amy, and Debra's siblings, Linda, Billy, Sandy and Tricia, their families and our daughter in law Rachel. I appreciate their love and value their support.

There have been so many other people that have been invaluable to me. Many coaches have worked with me to grow young athletes from boys to men. Their loyalty, friendship and hard work made it possible for me to be the coach I am. To Coaches Davidson, Hodnett, Williamson, Rippee, West, Walton, McChristian, Sides, Hogan, Wright, Lang, Briles, Holson, LeVallee, Cooley, Roark, Cook, Handley, Head, Lucas, Altoff, Pearson, Bell, Wasson, Schulze, Faith, Karger, Rodie, Brown and many others, I thank you for all you have done to make kids the best they can be. I also appreciate so many great administrators that have given me the support needed to run successful athletic programs. Thanks to men like Dr. Rees, Parsons, Lefever, Barker and Grusendorf for the chance to lead.

I want to extend a huge "Thank You" to Darren Hibbs and Stephanie Thigpen for their countless hours and incredible contribution in helping me write this book. Your talents and insights inspired me and have made this project what it is today.

Now in this new season of life, as I partner with the Flippen Group, their friendship and influence continues to be invaluable.

I cannot end without mentioning some great families that were strong influences on my family. To the James', Lesters, Kitchens, Millicans, Basons, Groves', Holubs, Andrews', Shipleys, and many others, I thank you. Special gratitude to the incredible women of my mom's prayer group that have been meeting every week for over 40 years to pray for their children. What a blessing they have been through the years.

I am most thankful and humbled for the grace of our Lord Jesus Christ who gave his life so that we might have a home in heaven and the power within us of the risen Savior. To Him, be all the honor and glory. He is and always will be the true essence of "Home Field Advantage".

INTRODUCTION
Roger Staubach

I have been blessed to receive a number of awards in my career. But for every accomplishment there have certainly been a number of failures and disappointments. As a matter of fact, some of my greatest victories came as a result of the lessons learned from my failures.

Adversity reveals genius; prosperity conceals it.

You find out about yourself when times are tough. I didn't get the nickname "Captain Comeback" playing for the Dallas Cowboys for no reason. There were numerous times where we executed poorly for three quarters and then pulled the game out in the closing minutes. The key to our success is that we never quit trying.

If you're going to achieve great success in life, you've got to start with a good plan and then execute well. You need to clearly understand your goals and be able to perform to the level of your objectives. Strive to give that extra. One of my favorite quotes is: "There is no traffic jam on the extra mile."

This probably sounds easy if you're in High School, or maybe a college freshman with your whole life ahead of you. But what about the rest of us? Is there still time to make our lives count? Is there time to make a mark, to leave a legacy for the next generation?

It doesn't matter how many failures you have had, or how many times you've underperformed in the past, there's always time to turn things around.

Is it time for you to make a comeback? The principles in this book, by my friend Brad McCoy, will inspire and motivate you to overcome every obstacle and persevere through every trial and fulfill your ultimate potential as a student, parent or coach.

It's not too late to call an audible. In the pages of this book are personal stories, insights and some of Brad's game-winning strategies for life. Whether you're just starting a career or trying to figure out how to get through to your 16 year-old, the lessons you will hone from this book will be invaluable.

> **Don't let excuses for past failures keep you from achieving greater success for you and your family.**

Home Field Advantage will help you identify some practical things you can do to perform better, achieve more and accomplish your goals.

So, whether you are just getting started in the game of life, or it's the two-minute warning, don't allow anything to stop you from making a difference in the lives of those you touch each and every day. Make every second count.

OK. Huddle up, the clock's ticking.

FOREWORD
By Troy Aikman

I met Brad McCoy in 2009 when we were both scheduled to speak to a group of educators. I was immediately captivated by his stories and insights on how to motivate young people. As a father and coach, he's seen the challenges of raising kids and athletes from a unique perspective. He has motivated hundreds of young kids to be winners both on and off the field.

My whole life I've been playing football or talking about it. When I was a student athlete I faced a lot of challenges. I'm thankful that I had voices in my life that steered me in the right direction. From a young age I understood that to be successful it took more than just talent.

Success requires hard work and discipline. And it's persevering in tough times that keep you there.

Persevering through difficult times is critical for every great leader to succeed. We went 0-11 during my rookie season with the Cowboys. That took a lot of perseverance to overcome the stigma that left—both in our minds and our fans. But hard work, good choices and a "never quit" attitude transformed us back into "America's Team." The same principles it took to transform the Cowboys are the same that can work for whatever team you're on. If you're head of a family, a student athlete, an aspiring musician or the CEO of a Fortune 500 company – these principles hold true.

Having the home field advantage in sports is a well-understood phenomenon. Does it mean you'll always win? Of course not. What it does mean is that all the things are in place to make it easier for you to succeed. You've got your own locker room, your car in the parking lot, and thousands of fans cheering for you instead of the other guy. It's the place you're most familiar with. That same principle is what we need to bring to every arena of our lives. Our home field advantage is the priorities and principles we take with us everywhere we go.

Living by a few well-defined and often repeated priorities will transform you. Whether you're looking to overcome the barriers that hold you back from going on to the next level of achievement or just trying to figure out how to get your kids to buckle down and work harder, Brad's words will encourage and challenge you to bring out the very best in yourself and those around you.

As you read this book, think about the principles, goals and priorities in your life. Are they setting you up for success or failure? Are they making it easier for you to make good decisions every day? Let Brad's experiences and advice guide you into greater success and give you that competitive edge that can only come from having the *Home Field Advantage.*

Home Field Advantage
Table of Contents

CHAPTER ONE

Far From Home

The scene was set. Not a cloud in the sky. 70 degrees with just a slight breeze. It had been the perfect day. It was Colt's day.

We sat in the stands that evening for the pre-game warm-ups with over 100,000 fans and watched as the band played, the flags waved, the fireworks boomed and fighter jets roared overhead. As dusk rolled in and the air force parachuters landed on the field I said a little prayer.

"Thank you, Lord. I couldn't have set this up any better myself. You made today perfect."

We'd watched Colt lead the University of Texas Longhorn offense a long way and this was the perfect culmination to a storybook season. Every first down, every completed pass and every touchdown celebration had us on the edge of our seats as we followed Colt that year. How fitting it was that his last game as a college football player was also the biggest of his career.

But it wasn't just Colt's night. This was also a family night for us. Colt's grandparents, parents, brothers, aunts, uncles and a fiancée were all there to watch their boy play on a national stage. We had all arrived a couple days early to take in the sights and sounds of the fanfare surrounding the Bowl Championship Series national championship game.

For us, the McCoy family, it was the culmination of a dream. Colt had wanted a national championship since he was a little boy and here we were. All of the chaos of fighting Los Angeles traffic before the game and fumbling with enough tickets for anyone who happened to be in Southern California that day named McCoy wasn't enough to take away from the moment. We breathed in the sights, sounds and the smells at the Rose Bowl as the Texas Longhorns kicked off to the Alabama Crimson Tide.

For me, this was a truly spectacular moment. I was so proud of Colt. He'd worked so hard to get where he was. The inner peace I'd felt all day through all the traffic and logistical headaches was magical.

There just wasn't anything that could take that away from me.

Total Control

I can't imagine any college football players not wanting to be in this game, but Colt's dream had come true. There are millions of high school football players in America. Of those, only 10,000 or so are starting quarterbacks. Of those, only a few hundred get chosen to play college ball and only a handful of them get to start for Division 1 schools. From that handful, only two get to be the starting quarterback in a national championship. Colt's lifelong dream of being that "one in a million" guy had come true.

Colt meticulously studied his opponents, so to say he felt prepared for the Alabama game was an understatement. When the Texas defense kept the Tide from getting a first down on their first drive of the game, Colt's jaw dropped as he watched them try a fake punt. I could hear his thoughts from his body language right then; "We're gonna smoke these guys!" The Longhorns would intercept the pass on the fake punt play, giving Colt great field position to start their first drive of the game.

As I watched I could tell he was in total control of his team. I always loved watching Colt play, and it made me happy to see how much fun he was already having. In four plays and a couple of first downs Colt had driven his team down the field into easy scoring position. Both teams were there because they were good enough to be there, but this was one of those games that from the first drive it seemed like everyone knew which way it would go. It was certainly shaping up to go in Colt's and the Longhorns' favor.

On the Longhorns' fifth offensive play of the game, Colt held on to the ball for an option play. Colt could really get yardage with his feet; it's what made him a hard target to defend. But before he'd gotten a few steps away from the center he took a shot from behind as he was heading toward the left sideline. It didn't look out of the ordinary, but something was different. He was slow in getting up.

Something's Very Wrong

I'd watched Colt play football for so many years that I could tell when something was different. The hit he took was definitely from a "big boy" but it wasn't surprising. All the boys on college football defensive lines were big. He didn't land on his head or anything; it just looked funny the way he went down. And I knew that as Colt's high school football coach I wasn't the only one who thought so. His mother knew something was wrong too.

I heard Debra gasp and whisper a prayer, "Please, Jesus."

That little prayer shook me. A hundred thousand fans were screaming and that whisper was the loudest thing in the stadium. I knew something didn't look right, but any time you hear a mother's desperate prayer for her boy, something begins to ache inside of you.

As Colt finally got up I saw him shake his head at Mack Brown, Texas' head coach, and tap his helmet as if to say, "Something's not right." I'd coached him since the 7th grade and in all my years I'd never seen Colt "tap out." He'd never taken himself out of a game before. He was a fierce competitor, so I immediately knew something was *very* wrong.

Football is a violent sport and you expect people to get hurt. You train and coach as hard as you can to prevent that from happening, or at least make injuries less catastrophic, but injuries happen. Colt was no stranger to them and I immediately thought this might be a flare-up of an old injury to his shoulder. His arm dangled at his side as if he'd pinched a nerve again.

It had been a couple seasons earlier Colt had taken a hit that resulted in an excruciatingly painful pinched nerve in his shoulder. It had healed just fine, but it was the first thing that ran through my mind as I tried to figure out what could be wrong.

The McCoy clan hadn't gotten to enjoy much of the first quarter before our euphoria had turned to nausea. Debra, as any mother would, was worrying about the health and safety of her boy. He was walking around, so we knew he was going to live, but a mother worries whether the next football injury will be her boy's last. As for me, I was in horrible pain. I knew Colt was okay, but I hurt to watch my competitive son on the sideline, helpless but to watch his team struggle.

They worked on him on the sideline for a while until they took him into the locker room for a closer evaluation. You'd think in a situation like that a player's parents would be kept in the loop as to what's going on, but that just isn't the case. Debra's and my phone were ringing non-stop with texts and calls from family members at home watching the game on television. They were feeding us the misinformed updates as they were coming to the announcers.

It was unbearable not to know what was going on. The pain raged inside my mind and my heart hurt. I knew what no one else in that stadium did; my son was dying to get back on that field and there was nothing I could do about it.

I only saw a couple minutes of the game that day. After Colt left the field my eyes were on the sideline. After he left the sideline my eyes were trained on the tunnel leading to the locker room. Then I just couldn't take it anymore.

I made my way down the stadium to the Longhorns' sideline hoping to find one of the coaching staff to let me on the field. As you can imagine, security is tight at these events and those security guards didn't know me from Adam, so they weren't going to let me on the field. But I caught the attention of one of the coaches and they signaled for me to come down. I raced through the tunnel and into the locker rooms.

Good Luck

As I approached the exam room I knew something was wrong. The team doctors were standing outside the room with a somewhat puzzled look on their faces. Colt had a great relationship with them, but he was in one of those "places" where he just wanted to be alone. He'd asked them to leave so he could deal with his situation. As I walked past them into the exam room the doctors looked at me with an expression of "good luck."

When I calmly walked through the doors into the empty room, Colt's head snapped up in rage as he glared at me, thinking I was one of the team doctors coming back in. When he saw it was me his eyes softened and his head and shoulders sank back down.

I don't know if you've ever seen a wounded animal or not, but there's a look in their eyes that tells you they've been broken but if they could get to you they'd kill you. My insides ached as I saw that in Colt. There was a fury about him as the thoughts raged inside his mind of working so hard only to have his moment taken away. I'd never seen him like this before and I was at a loss for what to do or say. Colt was always calm and collected. He really has a gentle nature about him, so this was new for me. But it was for him, too.

My son had worked so hard and achieved more than any quarterback in the history of college football. He'd won more games, scored more touchdowns and broken more records than anyone before him and here he was, all alone, listening to the muffled sounds of 108,000 fans above him watch the national championship game he was supposed to be leading.

This moment was all Colt had ever wanted and I was still hoping that he could get back in the game in the second half. I couldn't conceive of Colt being done after five plays. But Colt was now watching the game he'd dreamed of his entire life like millions of other Americans on television. I watched as the full range of emotions rolled over Colt like a flood what seemed like once a minute. I felt almost as undone.

I walked over to him on the exam table and threw my arm around him. His right arm was wrapped and packed with ice. It just hung there limp. He looked up at me with those wounded, angry eyes and just melted as he said, "Dad, I had 'em. I knew what they were going to do before they did it."

Halftime

At halftime the players started flooding in so I backed off to let Colt have his time with his team. Coach Brown came in and hugged Colt and shed a tear with him as he thought about this young man who'd led a team to a storybook game only to get taken out early on. Colt told him he was going back to help in any way possible. He said he couldn't throw it, but he could be a decoy or run the ball; he wanted to help any way coach would let him.

But Coach Brown had already talked to the doctors. He thanked Colt for all the things he'd done for the football program, but he wasn't going to put him back in and get him hurt any more than he already was.

Colt went and said a few things to the team. I could hear a few muffled things he said as he encouraged his team to rally around their new quarterback and get back into the game. As halftime ended the rest of the players went back out onto the sidelines and Colt came in the training room and looked at me and said, "Let's go. Come help me warm up." It was one of those moments as a dad that my insides just hurt. I still wasn't thinking he wasn't going to get back in the game, but I could see the anger and hurt in his eyes.

I prayed a quiet prayer and asked God to give him my arm. I didn't need it. This was his moment and I'd have done anything to help him run out of that tunnel and take his rightful place with his team and with this championship, and yet there wasn't a single thing I could do. The helplessness tore me up.

We went into a big, open room and Colt tore off the ice pack and gripped the football. He could barely hold up his arm under its own weight, let alone throw a football. He couldn't feel a thing, not even a needle prick.

Playing Catch

He threw it at me with such an awkward motion that the ball hit at my feet just fifteen yards away. It was as if he'd never thrown a football before and he had to think about every tiny motion his arm was making. It was like a right-handed person was throwing a ball with his left. He had zero control over his arm and his throwing motion.

I fought back the tears as I reached down to pick up the ball and as I stood back up I began to walk back toward him. It was obvious to me that he was done so I was going to give him a hug and tell him I was sorry. Before I could take two steps he angrily shouted at me, "Give it back!"

His anger set me on my heels. Colt was a fierce competitor, and he just couldn't bear the idea of not playing in that game. I knew that, but his anger surprised even me. I'd never seen him like this before.

I gathered myself from my shock and threw the ball back to him. But the young man I'd seen in the 7th grade throw a pinpoint pass 40 yards down the field couldn't throw a ball fifteen yards now. He tried to throw the ball another ten times or so and finally Colt sank as he realized it wasn't coming back. My heart felt torn into pieces to see him like that. There are no words to describe my emotions when I watched my son, who I'd never seen quit, have to concede the biggest game of his life to an arm that just wouldn't work.

People speak of seeing their lives flash before their eyes before a near-death experience. I wasn't physically dying, but something inside of me felt like I was. As Colt threw that ball so helplessly, memories of my young son flashed before me. The crowd above us roared as I choked back my tears and all I could see in that moment was my five year-old boy playing catch with me in the front yard; bright eyes dreaming and saying, "Daddy, daddy, I'm gonna win the Heisman!"

CHAPTER TWO

Being Intentional

Those two big, bright eyes looked at me with so many aspirations through the years. Well, six of those big, bright eyes did, actually. My three sons, Colt, Chance and Case were born competitors. They always had new goals and strategies to be the best at whatever they set their minds to. Whether it was an 8 year-old boy telling me he was going to have his own ESPN special or a 16 year-old young man proclaiming he'd have that ring someday, they were always thinking sports.

They came by it honestly. As a head coach and athletic director, football and sports almost always consumed our talk, especially at the dinner table.

We would come in from outside after a full contact game in the front yard. Whoever caught the ball tried to score versus the other two. There were never many penalties called. "No blood no foul" was our motto; so emotions ran high. If it ever did get out of hand Case and

I would take on the older two. I would throw or hand off to the little brother and then become his blocker. I think Colt and Chance would enjoy that more than anything. They could really unload the hits on their dad.

And I got beat up way more than I care to tell. But I loved it.

Those games were a regular occurrence when I would get home in the afternoon. It was usually after a long day and a tough practice so their energy level was always higher than mine but they would be suited out and ready to play the minute my truck pulled in the drive.

Whether it was from a trunk of unusable old equipment that I brought home from the field house so the boys could dress up like football players on Halloween, or the trademark Troy Aikman and Roger Staubach uniforms they had received under the Christmas tree the year before, they were always decked out and ready for me to put them through my team's regular stretching routine and get the games going. Usually they had their cassette player cued up with whatever was the latest "jock jam" beat that teams were listening to and would be "ready to rumble".

Often the boys would have convinced their mother to participate in the pregame preparation by helping them make a large banner they could run through at the start of the day's "big game". Debra was a great cheerleader. That is until the games got too violent. That was normally her cue to go in and get supper ready.

That front yard game would have to end at dark only because we didn't have stadium lights at home, although there were a couple of times I did move the truck into position where the headlights would light up the yard a little just to finish an overtime situation.

We didn't allow ties then, either. They were fierce little competitors, and it just wasn't an option. They didn't have a sister, so when I'd kid with them and say, "a game ending in a tie is like kissing your sister" didn't make any sense to them. But kissing anyone other than mom was "gross" at that time and for sure "not cool," so ties were simply unacceptable.

Those front yard super bowls would spill over into supper table rivalries. Who beat who, who cheated, who should have had a penalty, and the most common beef of all (except what was being served on their plates for the main course); "If Dad hadn't made that pass or thrown that block, yada, yada, yada!"

Chance would grin about the great one handed catch he had and then remind us all, especially his brothers, that no one was fast enough to cover him when he went long. Colt would fire back about the perfect pass he threw that Chance had missed that would have given them the title and the trophy for that day.

Oh, and yes, we had trophies...usually some huge old faded golden monstrosity that had been given to the basketball team in the 60's for the Lion's Club Tournament Championship and been thrown away 25 years later. I'd retrieved them from the dumpster during one of the gym clean-outs and polished them up for the winner of our front yard football classic championships.

Case would do his best to keep up with his older brothers but had a hard time getting a word in. He did hold his own, and since he and I did actually win more often than not he didn't take much of their trash talking. Trying to keep up with Colt and Chance really made him tough and escalated his high goals for success..."

It was so much fun...

Being Intentional

But sports do have to come to an end sometimes. Poor Debra would often have to put her foot down and declare that there'd been enough sports at the dinner table. It was time to talk about something else. Anything else. Something at school, something at church, just not sports. The four of us boys would sit in stunned silence for a while until we'd snapped out of it and remembered a non-sports related thing that had happened that day to talk about. It was hard sometimes.

She was right, though. We weren't going to let sports be all our family was about just because it came easy. It's not like Debra didn't like all the sports talk; she was a tremendous athlete and coach herself. She just wanted to make sure that there was more to our family than sports.

Debra would often make us change the conversation at the dinner table not because she was *really* tired of sports, but because she was being intentional about something else. And that was far more important to our family than who had dominated the game of the day.

We made the decision to do and say intentional things with our boys early on. We wanted to be able to take advantage of every opportunity with our boys to raise them right. And that meant being proactive and intentional. We had to have a plan.

If you're not intentional then things will happen by accident. There are a lot of things that happen spontaneously, some of them even good things. But most of the things that *just happen* aren't good. And even if they aren't bad, many times they're just distractions from what's best.

Being intentional is one of the most important things we can do as leaders, coaches and parents. If we have goals and priorities set beforehand we'll set ourselves up to take advantage of so many things. All too often we have missed opportunities because we weren't prepared beforehand with a way to take advantage of them. We must be ready to take advantage of every situation and that means being very clear with our kids. And I was thankful that Debra would ensure we made those dinnertime transitions with the boys.

That being said, we didn't put a lot of specific expectations on them. In fact, we only had one. We boiled everything we thought we could teach them day in and day out down to a simple, easy phrase to remember.

"Do your best and be a leader."

It may have been a simple phrase, but we said it to them every day. We said it every time the boys got out of the car to go into school. We said it every time we parted ways dropping them off just about anywhere.

We said it so often; in fact, that when the boys were older we rarely got to finish saying it before they'd slammed the car door and walked off. As they walked away from the car we would see them rolling their eyes and mouthing the last half, "Yeah, yeah, I know...and be a leader..."

We expected our sons to do their best in everything they did. We expected them to get good grades, stay out of the principal's office, be respectful to their teachers, help others who needed help and lead other people in their example. But we put those expectations on them by repeating that simple phrase that said it all.

Even if they were tired of hearing our little phrase we knew we'd done our jobs if it was stuck in their heads. We never told them to get straight A's in school. We never had to. It wasn't important if they got straight A's. What was important was that they did their best.

Did we have to question them sometimes when we knew they hadn't given their best? Sure! But we never had to make a long list of do's and do not's. They did walk the straight and narrow, and they did make the right decisions and lead others there (most of the time).

I wanted to keep things really simple and let the boys set their own goals, and that's why I chose the statement I did. The boys would often ask "what if?" questions. I'd tell them that if they had to ask then they probably weren't doing their best or being a leader. Having an intentional statement made it easy on Debra and I; and for the boys. One statement that we made on purpose every day said everything that needed to be said to launch our boys into excellence that day.

Setting Their Own Goals

I've enjoyed coaching and interacting with students, and it's one of my passions to see young people aspire to everything they can be. But I hung up my coaching hat in 2010 to go to work for a company that impacts students on a broader level.

The Flippen Group has given me the opportunity to interact with coaches and teachers all over the country and train them on how to more successfully reach their athletes and students with life-changing principles. It's something I love to do and I have the opportunity to reach so many more thousands of students now through their coaches and teachers.

At the Flippen Group we have a saying, "If you have too many priorities, you have no priorities." What we mean by that is if you start setting too many goals and giving too many objectives, it's too hard to decide what's important for that day. We were thankful we took this concept to heart with our sons.

Our boys became very good at taking their clear objective from their parents and making their own goals. One day while he was in high school Chance came to me and told me he was going to break the school pole-vaulting record. I hadn't ever encouraged him to break records. Debra and I never told any of our sons to try to be the best at anything; we'd only told them to do *their* best. So Chance deciding to break the school record was completely his own goal.

Chance had heard our mantra so many times by then he didn't need a pep talk from dad about working hard to achieve his goals. He knew that his only responsibility to us was to be able to look me, or his mother, in the eyes and truthfully tell us he'd done his best.

Chance worked hard for a long time. He worked out, practiced and made sacrifices to meet his own goal until the day he broke the school record. 14' 7" to be exact. It took a lot of hard work, but he stuck with it until he did it. He even went to the state track meet and medaled in the pole vault.

Our aim in not giving our sons a lot of stated goals wasn't because we didn't care if they did well in school. It was just the opposite. We wanted them to excel in every aspect of their lives but all too often we as parents place so many demands and artificial goals on our children that they can't decide what's the most important priority for today.

Reducing the number of stated priorities makes deciding what's important for that day so much easier. When everything you do can be boiled down to "do your best and be a leader" things become so much simpler. The questions get in your head. "Is what I'm about to do my best? Am I being a leader with this decision, or am I following someone that will cause me not to be my best?"

A lot of time my boys would ask me "what-if" questions.

"What if 'so-and-so' does this? What if I can't do this-or-that?"

I'd tell them if they had to ask too many "what if's" then whatever they were thinking about probably wasn't worth doing. If they had to ask "what if" too much they probably weren't doing their best or being a leader.

If you make a really intentional statement as a parent, then your children can be more intentional about their responses. There's not as much gray area to wonder about what you're doing. As a head coach I gave my coaches and players a very small set of simple principles that governed all our game plans and it made it very easy for everyone to execute. And more often than not our teams beat bigger, faster and stronger opponents.

Being intentional and having simple, clear priorities works on and off the field. It works in the classroom, the boardroom and the family room. Give people clear, simple goals and repeat them over and over again and you will be amazed at how people will make the best decisions by themselves.

Teachable Moments

One of the biggest reasons to have clear goals and well-defined priorities is it helps you take advantage of "teachable moments."

Teachable moments are those snapshots in time where all our repetitive statements can become real to kids. They don't come along every day, but when they do we have to jump on them. All too often we miss those moments because we're not prepared to act. If we're not prepared to act then we'll settle for something less than our kids' best and we spoil the moment.

When Colt was 6 years old I was the head football coach and athletic director in the little Central Texas town of San Saba. One of the great traditions they had there every summer was the rodeo. Colt came to me that summer and told me he wanted to ride a steer in a contest for little guys his age. The prize was a shiny "Texas-sized" belt buckle. Colt saw it and he was immediately captured by the idea of winning that belt buckle.

I didn't like the idea of Colt getting thrown off a small steer and I tried to talk him out of it.

"No, Colt, you're not going to like this."

"Please, dad! I really wanna ride," he pleaded.

"No, son, it's a little dangerous and you've never done it before. I don't think you're going to like it. It's not like you think it is."

"I know I could get hurt and that's okay. I wanna try," Colt begged.

Our banter went back and forth and finally he convinced me. But I told him if he signed up he was going to do it, no matter what. He emphatically said he was going to do whatever it took; he really wanted that belt buckle.

Really, I hoped he'd get thrown quick and it would all be over. I didn't think Colt was going to like it and Debra was even more against the idea of her little 6 year-old getting thrown from a steer, but if Colt wanted to do it I was going to let him learn his own lessons.

You may not have ever watched steer riding before, but it's 8 seconds of jerking, bucking, kicking and holding on for dear life. And that's the big cowboys. Now imagine a little guy on a little steer. It's 8 seconds of sheer terror, laughter, suspense and precious memories.

We had a great time that night visiting with all the parents of the other 15 or 20 knot-heads that were participating so we just didn't realize Colt had done as well as he had until the evening was over. He did very well, in fact, finishing in the top three. We weren't paying attention to how well anyone else's kids did, just to how Colt was hanging on.

I just wanted to be done with it all that evening, and making it to the finals meant we had to come back on Saturday night. But we were definitely going back because I made Colt give me his word he'd finish what he started.

When we arrived on Saturday night the steers were a little bigger and the crowd was bigger and Colt started thinking about what he had to do. I could see it in his eyes. The once fierce intensity of "Colt the competitor" had vanished and was replaced by something a little more star struck. About ten minutes before the competition was supposed to start he turned to his mother and said, "Momma, I don't wanna ride tonight."

My heart sank when I heard Debra say, "That's okay, Colt. If you don't want to ride tonight, you don't have to."

I knew I could have bit my lip and passed on the moment, but I just couldn't.

So I turned to Debra and said, "Yes, he does have to ride tonight. He said he'd do it and now he's going to do what he said he would."

She got a little frustrated with me and said, "But Brad, he could get hurt."

"Yeah, he might get hurt," I conceded, "but that's part of the deal." I looked at Colt with some tears starting to show and said, "Come on, let's go."

As I grabbed his hand and started toward the chute Colt came unglued.

"Daddy, daddy, please don't make me do it!" he shouted.

All the mothers there that night heard everything and they got really upset with me. They all knew I was the football coach and I could hear some of their indignant conversations with each other.

"That coach McCoy doesn't care about anything but winning."

"He's so bent on winning, he'll sacrifice his own son just to win."

As I took all this verbal abuse I climbed into the chute with a very upset Colt. The two cowboys at the chute looked at me like, "You've got to be crazy, coach McCoy!"

Now that's a hard thing to do, I have to admit. Colt was tugging on my heartstrings every time he tugged on my sleeve and asked me not to make him do it. I took no pleasure in forcing him to do it. I hated it, actually. I wasn't just the driven coach the accusing eyes were saying I was. My heart hurt for Colt.

And I especially didn't like setting my son on a snorting, mad-as-heck steer that didn't much care for him there either. But this wasn't about what Colt wanted. It wasn't about what I wanted, either. It was about what was going to make Colt into a good man someday.

I put him on that steer inside the chute with tears just streaming from his eyes. We men can callous ourselves to tears sometimes, but those tears hurt. But I had to stick with it. Those cowboys were still looking at me cross-eyed and with one last, "are you sure" glance they opened the chute and out Colt went, bucking and flopping about.

But Colt rode and stayed on the 8 seconds required. It wasn't the conventional way, though. He ended up sideways on the steer and after a somewhat brutal dismount the animal stepped on him. He had a busted lip and blood on his chin, but he was okay. And as you would expect, he finished first and won that belt buckle.

But I really didn't care if Colt won. I wasn't ensuring my place in the "doghouse" for a belt buckle, but so my son would become a man of his word. I wasn't willing to pass up on such a great teachable moment. Even though I slept on the couch a couple of nights...

Months later Colt came to me and thanked me for making him ride that steer. I asked him why it was such a big deal that night and why he decided he didn't want to ride. He told me he just got scared. He didn't even remember why he was scared, but he was. Nevertheless, he was glad I made him follow through with it.

It seemed like it was a relatively insignificant moment in a little kid's life, but it was one of those precious teachable moments that became important to Colt.

We have to take advantage of moments like that, as unimportant as a child riding a steer may seem. It was a moment that could have been a failure that we turned into a win. You really just can't overestimate the power of a moment.

Winning Moments

Sometimes it seems too hard to look for those teachable moments. There have been times in our lives where things were really tough. It would have been easier to coast through those situations and just come out "okay" on the other side. But I didn't want to waste those opportunities. We've had a lot of good times, but we know hardship too and there's never a good time to make excuses not to look for moments to turn losses into wins.

No matter how bad it is or how bad it gets, work to find "winning moments." Sometimes it doesn't seem like you have any teachable moments. But even if everything around you seems bad, find the positive things in the situation. Intentionally looking for those positive aspects are what can turn losing situations into winning moments.

Of course it really helps to have a plan so those moments don't pass you by, and that all comes back to being intentional. Ask yourself how much dedicated time you're taking to try to positively influence the lives of your kids, your students, your employees, or whoever it is you're mentoring. If you're not being intentional, you're probably not going to have the positive influence you'd like.

And even if things seem really hard and you don't feel like being intentional, there's always a way to find those "winning moments." Having a plan on how to be intentional sure makes it easier (not easy, mind you) to put your child on that "steer" even when they're begging you not to.

Coach's Pep Talk

1. Do your best and be a leader.
2. In real life, not everybody gets a trophy.
3. Do not follow where the path may lead, go instead where there is no path and leave a trail.

CHAPTER THREE

Keeping The Bar High

"I'm tired of suckin' it up," said Case, with tears dripping from his cheeks.

I didn't hear the response he mumbled into his soup because I was already down the hall; one of my assistant coaches sitting next to him at the teachers' table in the cafeteria heard him tearfully say it and told me later. But I wanted him to know I was serious. Lunchtime was over.

I'd brought Case with me to school that morning before he was old enough to attend. I'm not sure now exactly what the deal was, but I think Case was either upset about having to do something he didn't want to do, or about not being able to do something he wanted to do. But he was being especially slow that day at the lunch table and I'd told him it was time for him to finish his lunch and go. He didn't move much so I got a little agitated. I told him we had to go and it was time to finish his lunch.

He still didn't move. I had a busy day and I was only going to say it one more time.

"Come on Case, we have to go now. You've had enough time to eat. Suck it up and let's go!"

Suckin' it Up

All too often parents lose their way when their children are hurting and fall. The commitment to keep high standards for their kids wavers in tough situations, so they reach down and pull them up. They end up enabling children to fail because they don't want them to hurt. We're in a culture that's permeated with parenting that won't let kids experience success and failure on their own.

We can't make special circumstances for our kids because we feel things are "already too hard on them." By doing so we lower the bar for them at a critical time in their lives. When they are on their own no one's going to lower the bar. I was hard on Colt when he wanted to quit his steer riding competition, but I wasn't going to let him off the hook just because he changed his mind.

We have to keep our expectations for our kids high no matter what. There is nothing that we, as parents, should allow to come into our kids' lives that would in any way lower the bar of their potential. And sometimes that can be really hard...

Dirty Skin

Case was five years old the first time Debra noticed it. She was helping him finish up his evening bath when she spotted a small dirty patch on his leg.

"Surely this boy hasn't been in the tub for ten minutes and missed a spot," Debra thought to herself.

But when she did that mom "lick your thumb and wipe it off" thing, nothing changed.

"That's funny, it must be a scrape" Debra said. "Casey, how did you get this? Did you fall today?"

"No, Mama," Case replied.

Debra didn't think much more of it after that—I mean, you never know how a five year-old boy comes by the bumps and bruises and scrapes they bring home. She didn't think any more of it until it she found another one of the mystery rough patches. And another. And another.

After a few days of discovering these spots on Case Debra began to get worried. Something had to be wrong. She made an appointment with our pediatrician to figure out what was going on, but he thought it was just an unusual birthmark that sometimes appears on children Case's age. That didn't really sit well with Debra.

The truth is that Debra recently had a friend whose mother was diagnosed with a rare skin disorder that sounded like Case's problems. Then, a few weeks later, Debra saw a television special about some middle-aged women who had come down with the same thing. It was called *scleroderma (skler-oh-derm-uh)*. They'd wake up and seemingly overnight they had developed abrasive skin in different places on their bodies. Then the skin would get harder and stiffer. Debra was convinced this is what Case had.

By the time she took Case back to the pediatrician a few days later to have him take a look at some new spots that had developed, she was almost sick worrying about it. The pediatrician saw how upset she was, so he pulled her aside and asked her what was going on. She burst into tears and told him that she felt sure Case had scleroderma. The pediatrician couldn't really say for sure if that's what Case had or not, but he must have taken her mother's intuition seriously—he made an appointment for us three days later with a dermatologist in Abilene.

The dermatologist told us that the probability of scleroderma wasn't high because it was something rarely seen in children. He had to biopsy one of Case's spots before he could say for sure. The biopsy itself was an ordeal. Case got at least four or five shots in his back before they even took a sample.

We went back home and waited for the doctor to call us with results. It took about a week—a very tense and anxious week. When we finally got the call, the doctor confirmed what Debra already suspected.

Case had a form of scleroderma.

Our lives changed dramatically that day. But Sundays changed the most.

Any Given Sunday

It was the same thing every Sunday.

Debra and I got the boys out of bed, had breakfast, and went to church. If we didn't have anything special planned for the afternoon, we'd usually go back to the house and just hang out and relax. It seemed like the day always started out so great.

It was the night everybody dreaded—especially my youngest son, Case.

After dinner on Sunday nights, the mood around the house always changed a little. Debra would get kind of quiet. Colt and Chance usually found some way to disappear. Everybody knew what was coming.

We didn't always know from week to week how Case was going to feel. Sometimes, he was just kind of resigned to the whole deal. Even at the age of five—when we first started this routine—Case knew it was just something we had to do.

That's not to say he didn't try to get out of it occasionally, especially the first year or two. I can't imagine a kid who *wouldn't* under the circumstances. Those were the nights when the only way we got through it was kicking and screaming—when Case was literally begging and pleading.

"Please, Daddy, just wait until in the morning! Please don't do it tonight!"

It was gut-wrenching. There's really no other way to describe it. I would have loved nothing more than to grant him that wish.

The doctors had shown me how to do everything at home. I had to start by preparing the injection site with rubbing alcohol.

Case hated the smell of alcohol from the very beginning. I guess he always connected it to what happened after. He actually came up with some pretty unusual ways of dealing with the problem, one of which his brothers still give him a hard time about.

Whenever we'd get ready to start, Case would grab a box of Fruit Loops out of the kitchen. Then he'd sit there with that box of Fruit Loops in his lap and the second I broke out the alcohol, he would lean over and bury his nose in the box.

After I sterilized the injection site, I loaded up the syringe with medicine—a powerful chemotherapy drug called *methotrexate*—and flicked the syringe a couple of times with my finger.

Then I injected the drug into my son's arm.

Case's reaction was almost always instantaneous. Within a matter of just a few seconds, he'd get this look on his face like he just bit into something terrible. He always described it as an awful "flaky, metallic" taste. Then he'd run to the bathroom and get violently sick.

This happened every Sunday for probably three or four years.

Hard Skin

We would usually put a cool rag on his forehead until it was all over, and then put him to bed. He didn't always sleep so well on Sunday nights. The methotrexate was really hard on his little body. But it didn't slow him down much. He still got up every Monday morning and headed off to school—just like every other kid his age.

For the most part, Case *was* like every other kid his age—with one exception. Case had a rare autoimmune disease that literally caused his skin to "harden."

Scleroderma—which literally means "hard skin"—is an autoimmune tissue disease where, basically, the body makes too much collagen. This causes patches of skin to get really thick and rigid, like scar tissue. It also attacks tissues underneath the skin, like muscles, ligaments, and tendons as well.

We found out a lot about this disease in a very short period of time. We learned that there's more than one type of scleroderma. There's a scleroderma on the outside of the body and a scleroderma on the inside of the body. The kind on the inside—*systemic* scleroderma—can be fatal.

Doctors Say...

Thankfully, we learned early on that Case did not have the latter kind. He had what they called *localized* scleroderma, which is mostly on the outside of the body. The doctors told us it was very rare for localized scleroderma to turn into systemic scleroderma, but they didn't think it was impossible. So part of the goal in Case's treatment was to keep the disease on the outside of his body.

We were eventually referred to a specialist at Scottish Rite hospital in Dallas. Our great friends Kurt and Karen Parsons knew a doctor there who helped us get into the hospital quickly, for which we are eternally grateful. The doctor told us that because no two people with sclero-derma look the same, he couldn't really tell us for sure what was going to happen to Case. But he did give us a general idea of what to expect.

He said there would be quite a bit of scarring—some of it noticeable, some of it not so noticeable. The disease was probably going to slow down the growth on one side of Case's body, and he might have limited mobility in some of his joints because of the way the disease affects tendons and ligaments.

As for how long it was going to last, the doctor told us the disease would probably "run its course" in anywhere from five, to seven, to nine years. After it ran its course—or stopped progressing—Case would be left with whatever he was left with; meaning, we couldn't fix the damage that had already been done, but there probably wouldn't be any more new damage.

So all we had to do was help Case survive the disease for the next five, to seven, to nine years.

When we first got the diagnosis, Debra and I went through so many dif-ferent emotions those first few weeks and months. I think part of the problem was that, since Case was born, we had come to see our family as a family blessed with "three strapping, healthy boys." Then suddenly, in an instant, that wasn't our family anymore. We just didn't know how to deal with it.

But Case really helped us put the whole thing in perspective.

I'm Ready To Go To Heaven

We were driving home one night from a long day at the hospital when, out of the blue, Debra and I heard this small voice from the back seat.

"Am I gonna die?"

He sounded so matter-of-fact. It was almost like he was asking what was for dinner.

We were really caught off-guard. I can't remember now exactly how we answered him. I think we just reassured him that he wasn't going to die and that the doctors were doing everything they could to help him get better.

For the rest of my born days, I will never forget what that child said next. Even today, I can still almost hear him say it.

"Well, if God needs me right now, I'm ready to go to heaven."

Debra and I just looked at each other. I'm surprised I didn't run off the road. I mean, there we were—two 30-somethings still struggling to figure out how we were going to deal with this whole thing—and our five-year-old son seemed to have a better handle on it than we did.

For me, I think I just let my grown-up understanding—or lack of it—get in the way. I didn't understand why Case had to be sick; probably in the same way Case didn't understand how shots that hurt so much were going to make him better. As the adult, I knew the shots were part of a bigger plan that Case wasn't able to see or understand. And even though Case didn't understand the reason for it, he still trusted us to do what was best for him because he knew how much we loved him. I realized then I was going to have to do the same.

Hard Pills to Swallow

That trip was just one of dozens we would make to Scottish Rite over a period of seven years for testing and to check the progress of the disease. The trips to the hospital were tough, but Case was always a trooper. We'd pile everybody in the car usually about once a month—me, Debra, Colt, Chance, and Case—and head for Dallas.

Colt and Chance were still pretty young when we started making regular trips to Dallas—somewhere around 10 and 8. After the first couple of times, I think the novelty of it kind of wore off a little bit, and then they *really* didn't want to go anymore. In fact, I remember them literally begging us not to make them go. They even once asked him, "Case, you don't mind if we stay here, do you?"

Truthfully, I didn't blame them. It *wasn't* a lot of fun. But it also wasn't a lot of fun for Case. So staying home was never really an option. I made it clear to Colt and Chance up front that their little brother would need them—whether any of them knew it or not—to get through what was going to be a tough time. As a family, it was our job to support and encourage him. If Case was going to have to go through it, we were all going to go through it with him, as a family. Period.

And Case definitely went through a lot. It was unfathomable the number of times he got stuck with needles. Every time we took him to the hospital, they'd take four or five vials of blood so they could run a bunch of different tests. It just seemed like there were always needles everywhere. I really had a hard time taking it. I can't imagine how Case did.

The people at Scottish Rite were wonderful, though. It was their job to stick Case with all those needles, and Debra and I are forever grateful for the exceptional care and attention they gave him through the years. We're thankful for every wonderful doctor and nurse we had the privilege of meeting during our times there.

We knew pretty early on that Case would figure out a way to deal with all of this. I remember right after he was diagnosed, the doctor sent us home from the hospital with pills for him to take. They were pretty big pills, especially for a five-year-old who'd never had anything but liquid and chewables.

The first few nights, Debra tried to get him to swallow the pill with no success. It was pretty traumatic for both of them. On the third night, she was standing there trying to get him to take it when somehow the bottle got knocked off the counter and the pills scattered all over the kitchen floor. By that time, they were both in tears, running around frantically picking up pills off the floor.

Debra turned to Case and in total frustration said sternly, "You are going to take this pill!"

Then the weirdest thing happened.

Suddenly, Case's whole demeanor kind of changed. He looked at Debra through these big, red, puffy eyes and said, "Could you just go out of the kitchen please?"

She said "Fine," and walked out of the kitchen. Well, she didn't really walk out of the kitchen. She stood just outside the kitchen door where Case couldn't see her and watched to see what he would do.

The pill was in one of those little Tupperware cups sitting on the counter next to a glass of water and the bottle with the rest of the pills. Case stood there—in his underwear—on the other side of the kitchen, staring at that cup like it was high noon at the OK Corral.

Then all the sudden, he just kind of squared his shoulders, marched across the kitchen floor, and snatched the cup off the counter. He reached into the cup, pulled out the pill, and pinched it as hard as he could between his fingers. Then he tilted his head back, opened his mouth like a little bird, and stuck his fingers all the way to the back of his throat. After taking a big swig of water, he threw his head back and slammed the cup back on the counter. Then he turned and walked right past Debra and climbed into bed.

I think we knew right then that this kid was going to make it.

Coping

Case found a way to get by on his own, but we never let him do it alone. We were always with him. In fact, after we had been going to the hospital for a while and had gotten to know some of the staff there, they would occasionally start to run off with Case by himself to do some testing or something. Whenever that happened, Case would always give me that "Please don't leave me alone" look. So I always made it clear to the doctors and nurses that Case and I were a package deal—wherever he went, I went.

Sometimes Case would get really down about the whole situation. His hair had started to fall out and he was still getting stuck with needles all the time. He just couldn't make any sense of it.

We focused a lot on prayer, which has always been a cornerstone in my family. I prayed with the boys almost every night before they went to bed. For Case, that really became a time when he could kind of pour out his heart to God about everything he was feeling and struggling with, and turn over some of those burdens.

At other times he really blew us away with his ability to see the big picture. I remember times when we were at the hospital, Case would look around at the other kids and say, "God has blessed me. I'm not nearly as sick as they are. There are kids here that are really hurting."

As Case's disease progressed, he developed considerable scarring on his back, legs, and face. The left side of his body didn't grow and develop at the same pace as the right side, and he always had a lot of trouble with tissue pain in his left ankle.

And as the scars became more visible, Case had to learn how to deal with a lot of curiosity and questions from people.

I remember when he first started grade school; the doctors were still trying to find the best medicine to treat his disease. The first drug they put him on had a lot of side effects, including making him really sensitive to sunlight. So every time he went out on the playground, he had to wear long sleeves, a hat, and sunscreen. Then the doctors switched him over to another drug that suddenly caused him to lose a lot of weight and a lot of hair over a period of about six weeks.

With all this going on, his classmates were naturally curious. They always wanted to know, "What's wrong with Case?" His teachers usually answered that question with something like "Case has a skin disease." And they were always really good about telling the kids it was not the kind of disease they could catch. But "skin disease" is never a comforting answer for anyone. In fact, I remember one little girl went home and told her mom about Case, and her mom told her not to touch him.

Even the adults were less-than sensitive sometimes. I remember when the spots started showing up on Case's face, for the first few weeks or months they always made his skin look a little dirty. One Sunday, when one of the men at church saw Case, he came up to him and kind of licked his thumb and rubbed it on Case's face and said, "Boy, you need to wash your face."

Thick Skin

I know that kind of stuff was hard on Case. But, truthfully, he never was the kind of kid to feel sorry for himself. That's not to say he didn't occasionally. But when he did, we usually didn't allow it to go on for very long.

We never lowered the bar for Case just because he had a skin disease. He was expected to tow the line like everyone else in the family. We often used the motto "no excuses" in our family, which basically said we don't use excuses to get out of doing things we don't want to do.

Debra and I didn't always agree about how much I made him tow the line. She would say sometimes, "You're being too rough on him," or "He can't keep up," or "You're asking too much of him." And she definitely had great intuition into Case's limits. I just knew in order for him not to *feel* different, we had to try not to *treat* him different.

Honestly, the Dad in me never wanted to be hard on Case. I would have just as soon not made him do all the hard stuff everybody else had to do. I mean, he had already done more hard stuff in his short life than most people do in a lifetime. The Dad in me wanted to shield and protect him. But I think the coach in me knew that if I lowered the bar for Case—if I expected less from him—then if the disease didn't handicap him, I sure would.

When Case mumbled into his soup he was "tired of suckin' it up", that nearly killed me. I knew he was tired—that little boy was just flat worn out. I have no doubt at that moment he felt like he'd taken about all he could take.

Even though I could be harder on him than I wanted to be sometimes, there was also a lot of love and affection between Case and I.

Broken Records

When Case was really young and had just been diagnosed with scleroderma, Colt was just starting junior high and Chance wasn't too far behind. They both loved their little brother a lot and it hurt them to see Case go through the kinds of things he had to go through. At the same time, they were also just regular kids who wanted to do regular kid things, and not have to hang around doctors and hospitals all the time. And, since we didn't tell either one of them in the beginning how serious Case's illness really was, I think sometimes they thought Debra and I were making too big a deal of the whole thing.

The disease made Case a little more physically vulnerable when he was younger, so I asked Colt and Chance not to hurt him. I also told them it was their responsibility to take up for Case if anybody ever gave him a hard time. Most of all, I asked them to love him as much as they possibly could and show it as often as possible.

They didn't always understand why they were asked to do the things they did, but they did it anyway, which Debra and I always appreciated. As Case got older, it really meant a lot to him too. Colt and Chance became great mentors for Case.

And Case was always challenged by his brothers. He always wanted to do everything they did. He never wanted to be left behind. If they could do it, he wanted to do it better. From as early as I can remember, he believed he was just as strong and just as capable as anyone else.

We also tried to surround Case with as many positive messages and words of encouragement as possible. In fact, it seems like now I must have said these words to Case a million times: "Be thankful. God has a plan for you. It's gonna make you better. It will make you stronger. If you can beat this, what can't you beat?"

I'm sure if Case had known what a broken record was, he'd have thought I sounded like one.

When I Go Pro

And there was always a lot of affection to go around in our house, which I think may have helped Case most of all. Debra made a huge contribution in this area. She always went out of her way to show all three of our boys how much they were loved and adored.

I remember not too long after Case was diagnosed, as part of his therapy, Debra would have to put lotion all over him when he got out of the tub, and then massage and rub and stretch the lesions and the surrounding skin. While she was doing that, she would always say things like, "I love you. I love this spot. I love every one of your spots."

As Case got older and the disease started taking a more visible toll on his body, he not only had to deal with questions from friends and classmates, but he also had to deal with questions of his own, like, "What am I gonna look like when this is all over?" and "Are there things I won't be able to do that other guys can?"

I remember it was about that same time period when Case and I were watching some kind of feature on ESPN about an athlete who had overcome terrible circumstances. I'll never forget Case looking down at some of his scars, and then looking up at me and saying, "Dad, when I go pro, I'm gonna have a story to tell just like that guy."

No More Shots

When Case was 12, the doctor finally gave us the news we had waited seven long years to hear.

"We don't want to use the word 'remission,'" he said. "But it kind of looks like that's where we are."

That was it. That's what we needed to hear. The disease had finally stopped.

We knew there would always be a possibility that more lesions could appear later. But for Case, there was really only one important question.

"Do I have to get any more shots?"

His doctor smiled. "No, Case. No more shots."

Man, you'd have thought the McCoy family just won the Super Bowl.

Today, Case has a lot of scars on the outside of his body and they have changed a lot over the years. They mostly look like burns now. His hair is a little thinner on the left side and he doesn't have much of an eyebrow there. He has no hair on his left arm or left leg.

As far as the impact on his growth and development, basically everything on Case's left side is slightly smaller and less developed. His right foot is a size 12 and his left foot is a size 11, and his left leg is a little bit thinner.

But Case hasn't let it slow him down any. He's worked really hard to compensate for what the scleroderma took away. On the outside, the disease did some damage, but on the inside, it really fortified him. It gave him inner strength, self-discipline, a strong work ethic, perseverance, and an unbelievable will to win.

Robbing Our Children

We could have seen Case's disease for the life-threatening situation it was and cut him some slack along the way. We could have made it easier on him so many times because of what he had to go through, and there's not many days I wasn't tempted to do so. But we would have robbed Case of his ability to succeed. We would have given him something less than we'd given his two older brothers.

We didn't know how long Case would have the disease, so if we'd put his life or ours "on hold" at any point along the way, we would have lost 7 of his most formative years. All too often parents cave in to this and they steal from their children the great lessons of life children need to learn.

We couldn't let ourselves rob Case of his future just because it would have been easier on our spirits along the way. Every Sunday I wanted to find a way out of giving him those shots. But I knew he had to have them if he'd have a chance at living. In the same way, it was a struggle to keep the bar held high for Case, but every day I had to remember he needed Debra and I to keep that bar high to have a chance at winning in life.

And winning is just what he's been doing lately. His junior year in high school, he received offers for football scholarships from the University of Texas, Texas A&M, Arizona, Auburn, Colorado State, Florida, Florida State, and Nebraska, to name a few. His senior year he led Graham High School to the 3A State Championship Game and was named to several All State teams. He committed to the University of Texas Longhorns and won the back-up quarterback job as a true freshman.

Case may just get to tell that story after all.

Coach's Pep Talk

1. Most people's problem is not that they aim high and miss but that they aim low and hit.
2. No organization can rise above the constraints of its leadership.
3. Don't limit your challenges; challenge your limits.
4. Prepare the child for the path, not the path for the child.

CHAPTER FOUR

Priorities

I'll never forget it. We were sitting in a restaurant outside of Dallas when Colt made the announcement.

It was the summer after 6th grade and we were on our way home from visiting Debra's parents in Arkansas.

Everybody was just about done eating, when out of the blue Colt grabbed his half-finished soda, gulped it down, banged the glass back down on the table, and said,

"That's it. That's the last Coke I'm gonna drink."

He's just trying to be funny, I thought.

I started to call his bluff by saying something like, "That wasn't Coke. That was Dr. Pepper." But when I looked across the table at him, I could see he wasn't kidding. (Besides, anyone who's ever spent more than a week in Texas knows that Texans call all soft drinks "Cokes.")

I gave Debra my best "Did-you-know-about-this?" look, but I could tell she was just as surprised as I was. Chance and Case just sat there with their mouths open, waiting for the punch line.

I honestly couldn't think of a reason—short of the threat of bodily harm—that a 12-year-old kid would voluntarily swear off of Cokes. Maybe he didn't mean permanently. Maybe he just meant like "the last Coke today" or something.

"You mean, the last one you're gonna drink, ever?" I asked.

"Ever," he said emphatically. "I'm quitting for good."

While the hallelujah chorus was going off in my head, I asked, "So... what made you decide that?"

Debra and I—both coaches and former athletes—had spent years preaching to the boys about the importance of taking care of their bodies. In fact, they'd heard my "put the right fuel in your tank" speech so many times they could probably recite it by heart.

"I want to be a better athlete," he said, matter-of-factly.

I found out later that his decision probably had less to do with my preaching than it did with a motivational speaker he had recently seen who got him all fired up about making healthy choices. But, hey, he got the message!

I was proud he had made the decision on his own. I wanted to be supportive and encouraging, but at the same time, I also wanted to challenge him a little bit.

"I don't know, Colt," I said, kind of shaking my head. "That may be pretty tough. I guess we'll just have to wait and see."

"I can do it," he said, probably reassuring himself as much as he was me.

"Okay then!" I said. "I'm gonna do my best to hold you to it!"

And so it began.

The Temptation

Colt didn't drink any more sodas that day. He didn't drink any more sodas that week. Before I knew it, weeks had turned into months. It quickly got to the point if you saw a glass in Colt's hand, it was a safe bet that the only thing in there was milk, juice, or water.

I was really kind of blown away. I mean, ever since I can remember, I've been a Dr.-Pepper-aholic. Even as an adult, I'm not sure I could give them up. I can't imagine how hard it must have been for a 12-year-old.

Debra and I tried not to make it any harder on him than it already was. Fortunately, we weren't in the habit of keeping soft drinks around the house, which probably had more to do with finances than our health.. As a family of five struggling to make it on one income, it was pretty hard to beat the price of water.

So Colt didn't have to worry too much about carbonated temptations at home. He just had to worry about them everywhere else—in a world literally saturated with soft drinks.

I started sharing Colt's story with the high school football players I was coaching at the time—a story about "this 7th grader down the street" who was so committed to being a better athlete that he gave up all things carbonated. The story got circulated so much when Colt was in junior high that by the time he got to high school, it was already the stuff of small-town legend.

Then it really became a test for him. Kids were always waving soft drinks under his nose trying to tempt him. Some of his friends even tried slipping a little Sprite in his water when he wasn't looking.

But the harder people tried to trip him up, the more determined he got. From a very early age, Colt was his own guy. He didn't care too much what other people thought. I mean, he cared what they thought of him as a person, but peer pressure wasn't really a big deal for him.

Colt will be the first to admit that he was tempted. He may have given up sodas, but that didn't mean he still didn't want them. In fact, I remember quite a few times when somebody would be drinking a soda, Colt would lean over and take a big whiff of it and go, "Mmm. That smells so good."

I think at some point it just became a matter of principle for him. Colt was a smart kid. He knew that drinking a little flavored sugar water wouldn't suddenly make him a bad person or a bad athlete. I think it became symbolic for him—a symbol of his commitment to do whatever it took to be the best athlete he could be.

Ten years later, that commitment hasn't changed. He still hasn't had a "Coke."

Over the years, people have asked me how I thought Colt was able to make that kind of commitment and stick to it when he was so young. I have no doubt there may be some people who think I put him up to it. Honestly, I'd be happy to take the credit, but this was totally Colt's deal.

The fact was, Colt loved soft drinks. And he loved football. He just happened to love football more. His goal—his priority—was to be a champion football player. He knew soft drinks wouldn't help get him there, so he gave them up.

It was that easy—and that hard.

Not everything we have to give up in life is about making choices between good things and bad things. I suppose the argument could be made that soft drinks aren't "good" for your body, but really in the grand scheme of things they're not that bad when drunk in moderation. Colt wasn't really giving up something bad for something good—he was giving up something of lesser value to achieve his goal.

Many times in life we have choices between two good things. When we have the option to give up something good that's of lesser value to us, we should choose what's better in the long run for our goals and priorities. We should ask ourselves, "Is what I'm doing the *best* thing I can be doing?"

Sometimes good can be the worst enemy of what's best.

Living Priorities

Practically from the time Colt was old enough to walk he wanted to play football (probably not a huge surprise...he was a coach's kid).

But I explained to him early on that wanting to play didn't necessarily mean he'd be good at it. I told him he would be competing against other guys—a lot of whom were bigger, faster, and stronger—who had the same dream he had of playing college or professional football. I tried to help him understand that if he wanted to make his dream a reality, he was going to have to set some priorities—to decide what was most important to him—and then work and sacrifice harder than anyone else to get there.

That's exactly what he did. It wasn't some kind of fairy tale where a small-town Texas quarterback magically becomes a Heisman Trophy runner-up. His success wasn't handed to him on a silver platter. In fact, nobody really knows the price Colt has paid to get where he is. That boy has worked hard and sacrificed a lot along the way.

And it wasn't just soft drinks. He gave up a lot of other things too. A lot of times when his buddies from school were out having fun, Colt was busy training and working out. When they were out until midnight or 1 o'clock in the morning, Colt was usually home in bed. When they went out drinking and partying, Colt found something else to do.

That's not to say he had no social life. He did. But for the most part, if the decision was between his social life and his priorities, his priorities usually won out.

Sure, some of the kids gave him a hard time about it. I even coached a few of them. They'd try to talk him into doing things he knew he shouldn't be doing. They'd say, "Aw man, get real. You don't have to do everything your Dad says. I mean, he tells us the same thing."

But he managed to stay the course for the most part. I honestly think a lot of it had to do with the fact that Colt had a vision for what he wanted to be and he always tried to keep that vision in front of him.

It's not always easy for kids to "get ahold of" what it means to set priorities and make sacrifices. I've always said that you can tell a person's priorities by the way they spend their time and their money.

But Debra and I learned early on that talking about priorities and living them are two different things. We could talk about what was important until we were blue in the face, but if our kids didn't see us living it, it really didn't mean much. So we always made setting and sticking to priorities a pretty big deal.

We tried as much as possible to measure our family life by those standards and involve the boys in that process. When we had stuff come up that we found ourselves spending a lot of time and money on that were interfering with other things that were important to us, we always tried to ask the question, "Is this one of our top priorities?" If it wasn't, then we tried to readjust our focus a little—spend less time and money there. We definitely didn't do it perfectly, but we tried to keep that as the goal anyway.

Top Priorities

In our home, the top two priorities were always faith and family--those were pretty much non-negotiable. Academics came third and football and sports came fourth. You can bet those could be a challenge to keep in order!

As part of our faith priority, church was always important. In fact, I remember one time taking Colt and Chance camping with me in central Texas (Case wasn't quite old enough yet). We were going to spend the weekend fishing on the Colorado River. By Sunday, we'd pretty much caught all we were going to catch, so we packed everything into the truck and headed home.

Driving back through one of the small towns along the way, we passed a little church that looked like it was getting ready for Sunday services. I thought it might be kind of neat to drop in on their service and worship with them, so I turned into the parking lot.

"Aw, Dad. We're not going to church like this, are we?" Colt asked, obviously exasperated. He had that "you've-got-to-be-kidding-me" look on his face that kids are so good at.

I looked at the boys' clothes. They were wearing pants they'd had on for most of the weekend—the very same ones they were wading around the river in, and probably the same ones they'd wiped their hands on after baiting their hooks. Their shirts, which looked slept-in (probably because they were), were covered with the usual "camp grime"—some campfire soot, a few fish scales, and some Doritos smears. Their hair was flattened in a ring around their heads from the baseball caps they'd had on all weekend.

I have to admit, Colt and Chance had definitely looked better. It had been three days since any of us had seen the inside of a bathtub. But, I figured God wouldn't mind if we were dirty and smelly. I just hoped the folks inside would feel the same way.

"You're fine, Colt," I said, opening the door. "There's nobody you know in here anyway. C'mon. Let's go."

As we got to the front door, I turned and looked at Colt and Chance coming up behind me. Their faces were kind of bunched up and their heads were sitting really low on their shoulders. They looked like turtles trying to disappear into their shells. I'm sure they were imagining some big scary room full of people all pointing and laughing at them.

But it was quite the opposite. When we walked in the door of the church, you'd have thought we were royalty or something. These people didn't know us from Adam, but they welcomed us like long lost relatives. In a town of probably 1,500 people, they were probably just excited to have visitors at all—regardless of how they smelled. I think even Colt may have ended up having a good time. I know Chance and I sure did.

Our Work Here Is Done

Now that our kids are out of the house, Debra and I can't really set priorities for them anymore. But I have to say it's been really neat to watch them begin setting their own priorities.

I remember Colt's first year as quarterback at the University of Texas when the Longhorns played Kansas State. Things had been going pretty well for the Longhorns that season. They were ranked in the top 10 nationally and Colt had been having a lot of personal success as well.

In the opening drive of the game, Colt had three or four really great passes, but then things kind of stalled out, so Texas ran an option play on 2nd down. From where I was sitting, it looked like Colt made it into the end zone, but the officials ruled him down on the one-inch line.

On the very next play, Texas ran a quarterback sneak. Colt was able to dive into the end zone and score, but just as he did, one of the Kansas linebackers hit him pretty hard in the shoulder and neck area.

While everybody was busy celebrating the touchdown, I was staring at the pile of players on the field. I could see the bottom of the pile wasn't moving, which is never a good sign. Finally, I saw Colt get up, but I could tell by his posture and the way he carried himself off the field that he was hurt pretty bad.

The team's doctor took a look at him when he came off the field. Colt was in excruciating pain and had no strength on the right side of his body (which we later found out was an impingement, or pinched nerve). They worked on him for a while, but he was never able to get back into the game.

Texas ended up losing the game by a couple of points, which knocked them out of the top 10, and Colt had the first serious injury of his college career.

After the game was over, the Kansas State fans went nuts—it had been a long time since they'd beat Texas. They started flooding the field. I could see Colt standing out there with his arm in a sling looking shell-shocked and getting knocked around a little by all the crazy fans. So I went over the wall along with the rest of the Kansas State fans and ran out to him on the field.

It was kind of a surreal moment. We were out there with what seemed like 80,000 people rushing the field and I'm looking at Colt standing there, badly hurt giving me that same look like he did when he was three as to say, "Dad, why'd this have to happen?"

It turned out to be an incredibly long night in Manhattan, Kansas.

The team flew back later that night and got back into Austin in the wee hours on Sunday morning. I'm sure it wasn't a fun flight home. Colt was still really hurting. The team was bitterly disappointed. I'm sure the coaches were upset and frustrated too.

About a week or two after the game, I got a note in the mail from a man in Austin. He told me that he and his seven-year-old son were both big U.T. fans and that they had both stayed up and watched the Kansas State game on TV that Saturday night. They knew Colt had been hurt pretty badly and that the loss was probably really disappointing for him.

But the man said when he and his son went to church the next morning, just as they were about to sit down, Colt walked in—arm in a sling, obviously still in a lot of pain—and sat down a few rows in front of them.

"We knew he was beat up and exhausted," the man wrote. "But there he was, in church. You can't imagine what a life-changing impression he made on my son."

Since then, I've gotten lots of comments from people—who call, send emails, and stop me after football games—about how much they appreciate Colt being a role model for their children.

I have to say, it's pretty exciting to see your son conduct a last-second drive to win the Fiesta Bowl or be a runner-up for the Heisman Trophy. But when I hear about the positive impact he's had on other people just by being a good person and setting a good example, that really makes me proud.

It means a lot to see our priorities becoming our children's priorities as they get older. When I got that letter after the Kansas State game, it was obvious that Colt was willing to make the sacrifices necessary to keep God a priority in his life.

No Sacrifice

Oftentimes people talk about making sacrifices for their kids or their spouses or their goals. I don't think Colt would see giving up carbonated drinks as a sacrifice now. They were just something that didn't line up with his priorities.

A sacrifice is something that you make when you give up something of equal value for something else. That may not be Webster's definition, but it's what rests in my mind. I think if Colt had been forced to choose between a career in football or baseball—that might have been a sacrifice. Giving up soft drinks for football was not!

Debra and I gave up a lot along the way for our kids. I had opportunities to get my foot in the door as a coach at the college level. I had opportunities to coach at larger metropolitan Texas schools as well, but I turned them down, not because I didn't want a career in football, but because they didn't line up with our priorities. Our first priority was our children. Football always had to take a back seat to that.

Do I think that if I had fully pursued my coaching career that I'd be coaching against Joe Paterno and Mack Brown? I doubt it. But even if I had been good enough to make it to that level it wouldn't have been enough to entice me away from my priorities. I never felt like I sacrificed a better career for my family. Coaching at medium-sized high schools offered me the perfect opportunity to be involved in my kids' lives while making a difference in the lives of many other kids. That's not to say that coaches who choose to coach in large cities or in college have no priorities or can't raise strong children. I'm only saying those things didn't fit my priorities.

My good friend Flip Flippen says that a short-term loss for the sake of a long-term gain is a no-brainer. Investing time now in our children will pay huge dividends when they are out making their own decisions. At the time giving up job offers and opportunities may have seemed like a loss, but in the end I feel I gained a lot more. Colt, Chance and Case will always have to make their own decisions, but I know that Debra and I did everything we could to make them men of integrity and character. Ask any man, great or small, and he'd honestly tell you that's worth more to him than all the fame and fortune he could have acquired.

Real Priorities Are Lived Priorities

Kids have to see that our priorities are real. They have to be more than lip service. We really can't fake our priorities. They definitely have to start with us saying them, but we also have to show them to our children. Kids have a much easier time understanding and setting their own priorities when they see them modeled. It's not enough to have priorities; we have to actually live them.

Living them in front of your kids is important, but that means you have to live them in front of the mirror first. All the times when we realized our priorities had slipped out of order were hard because they had probably been replaced by something we liked. But we knew we had to change things when they were out of order. And that's more important than anything else—not that you live your priorities perfectly, but that you make the necessary adjustments when you find that you're not.

There were plenty of times that happened to us along the way, and I'm proud to say that my wonderful wife was often our barometer. She would bring our family back on track when we were veering off our path.

There were many times, especially when Colt and Chance got older, where it would have been easier to leave them at home when we took Case to Dallas to see the doctor. But our second priority was family, and we kept with it. We were sticking together, no matter what. Case needed his brothers, and since they knew what our priority was they rarely even complained about the daylong road trip once a month. It became so much a part of us that even when Case offered for his brothers to stay home, they wouldn't accept.

Now our boys are as close as they could be. They love and support each other in good and bad times. I love it when I find out a week after the fact that Colt called Chance to give him some advice and cheer him up about a hard loss or when Case calls Chance for some older-brotherly advice and encouragement. We made family our priority and now its theirs, all on their own.

But our family priorities may not be yours. Or they may not be in the same order as yours. Whatever yours are, be intentional about living them and staying on track with them.

There may be things along the way you have to give up to keep your priorities in order. Like Colt we may have to give up a little sugar water along the way, but we'll probably never miss it. The things Debra and

I gave up never felt like sacrifices because what we gained was so much better.

We've never missed them and we never will.

Coach's Pep Talk

1. Your priorities are evidenced not by what you announce, but by what you become.
2. A vision that doesn't act is nothing more than a daydream.
3. Success usually comes to those who are too busy to be looking for it.
4. I can't hear what you're saying because your actions are so loud.

CHAPTER FIVE

No Excuses

I knew my athletes could perform better. My problem was figuring out how to get it out of them.

I mean, I had done everything right in my mind. I'd worked hard to develop a good playbook. We were conditioning the boys well. We practiced hard. But it just wasn't coming together.

I had been an assistant coach for a couple years in San Saba, Texas and I had just become the head football coach for that season. Every coach knows in the back of their mind that it's hard to get good performance out of your athletes in your first season, but no one wants to accept a losing season. Not even if it's your first. I just didn't want to believe it was happening to me.

Every coach dreams of the day that they get their first big shot on top. You know that mentality; "I'd never been the head coach before but I

was sure I'd know how to do it better than anyone else once I got there."
Yep. I was there for sure.

The problem is that when reality sets in--when you suddenly realize
you're not automatically the best coach ever--that's when the temptation arises to give up. That's exactly what my athletes had already done.
Things weren't going how they thought they would so they were just
"checking out." They had, for all intents, quit on me. It was up to me to
decide whether our season was over.

We were just about to start district play, so it was a crucial time for our
team. If we could pull things together we could make a great season. If
we gave up, then we were surely in for a long season. Once a team has
truly given up, things get miserable quickly.

I knew I had to do something out of the ordinary to get their attention.

The Rock

I told my coaches to bring their wives over to my house that next Saturday night. A couple of them weren't married, and I told them they had to
bring a date, so they'd better find one. Or I would. At practice I told my
athletes the same thing. But for them I made the rules a little more strict.
If they were dating someone at the school, then they could bring her. If
they weren't, they had to find someone who wore a uniform and bring
her. It could be a member of a sports team or a cheerleader or a band
member. It didn't matter to me but if they couldn't find a date I would
find one for them (I was a real matchmaker).

I guess they took my matchmaking threat seriously because everyone
came with a date that met my demands.

My coaches and athletes weren't used to being invited to a social event
at their coach's house, so everyone was expectedly awkward at first. I
knew I was going to have to do something that would break the ice. A
bunch of teenage boys at their coach's house with...gulp...a bunch of

teenage girls—I knew I had to come up with something good. The burgers we grilled worked okay, but I knew it would take more than a little food to get people to come out of their shells. And I needed them out.

While I was clearing out my yard getting ready for everyone to come I was thinking about what to do for an icebreaker when I stumbled upon it. It just caught my eye. It was kind of flat on one side and all the edges on it had been worn smooth—like it had tumbled around in a riverbed for a while. It wasn't huge, but it was surprisingly heavy. We had lots of rocks in our yard, but this one caught my eye. I mean, it was just a rock, so it didn't look that interesting, but I had a great idea when I saw it.

Nothing makes teenage boys forget their surroundings like a good competition. Why not pit them against each other to see who could throw the silly rock the farthest? I picked it up and set it aside for that evening with my clever plan in mind.

After everyone had finished their burgers I brought it out. Things were still very awkward but everything changed when I explained the challenge. There was no prize for whoever tossed it the farthest--there didn't need to be. Bragging rights in the locker room were enough. But boy, did those guys ever forget their surroundings.

It was "on" almost instantly.

During the contest, it was kind of funny to watch the guys come up with different ways to throw a big rock. Some of them picked it up with one hand and flung it like a shot put; others picked it up with two hands, and then turned around and pitched it backwards over their heads; then there were those who picked it up with two hands, dangled it between their legs, and then swung it over the throw line (kind of like those little kids you see at the bowling alley).

The kid who won the competition really surprised us. His name was Kenny. He wasn't the biggest guy on the team. In fact, he was a running back who was actually a little on the small side. He was pretty quiet and mostly kept to himself.

Kenny was declared the official winner after the assistant coaches marked and verified the distance on his throw using plastic forks left over from dinner as the "measuring tape."

I remember watching him when all the kids were crowding around him, whooping and hollering, and high-fiving. I swear it was like somebody flipped on a light switch in that kid's eyes. He was instantly the hero for the night.

In fact, everyone seemed so excited about the whole rock-throwing thing that I wanted to make a bigger deal of it than I had originally planned to. So I ran into the house, grabbed a Sharpie, and asked Kenny to sign his name on the rock. We even took a picture of him with it, which ended up in the town newspaper that week.

I was glad the kids had so much fun with the rock-throwing competition because the next activity I had planned, which I hoped would be the most meaningful of the night, probably wasn't going to be as much fun.

I made everyone move over to the part of our yard where I had set up a fire. They knew pretty quickly we were moving from the fun of the rock-throwing contest to something a little more serious. I gave them all little slips of paper and had them sit down.

Pointing The Finger

The football season we were in was definitely a tough one. We had been winning games, but just by the skin of our teeth. I knew these guys were not committed to giving their best effort to winning football games—for a lot of reasons.

The whole purpose of this little exercise by the fire was to figure out what those reasons were.

It seemed like everybody and their brother had an excuse for why we weren't playing better. The kids said so-and-so wasn't playing well because he was too serious with his girlfriend. Teachers said so-and-so wasn't playing well because he was having trouble in class. Parents said so-and-so wasn't playing well because he didn't like his coach. Coaches said so-and-so wasn't playing well because he didn't have the skills.

If you asked so-and-so why he thought he wasn't playing well, there was a good chance he'd turn around and point the finger at another so-and-so on the team.

There were so many excuses for why we weren't doing better, and I knew it was the excuses themselves holding us back.

Whose Fault Is This?

Before I had handed out the slips of paper to everyone I made them listen to me for a little bit.

I said, "Okay guys. So, we know things haven't really gone like we planned this season. Right?"

I saw a few heads nodding. The rest just had that tail-between-their-legs look.

"And do you know whose fault that is?"

I suddenly saw about 30 heads drop. Everyone was intensely studying their laps.

"It's mine," I said. "That's right. It's my fault. And I want you to know I take full responsibility."

A few of them started to disagree.

"No coach! It's not your fault!"

"Yes, it is. It's my job to motivate you guys to win football games and I obviously haven't been doing my job. I've made excuses too and blamed other people for stuff that I could have handled better."

They all kept looking at each other like, "Is this guy crazy?"

"Remember at last week's game when Kenny fumbled the ball and I got all over him for it?" I asked. "I was wrong for that. I called a bad play and we hadn't practiced it enough. I shouldn't have put him in that position."

"So, am I the only one? Do any of you guys ever make excuses for not doing your best or maybe blame somebody else for stuff you did wrong?"

That question got everyone to studying their laps pretty intently.

Are You A Deer Hunter

So we talked about excuses a little bit—about the reasons we come up with for not doing our best. We talked about physical excuses, like not taking good care of our bodies, and not investing the time and effort necessary to train them to perform well. We talked about relationship excuses—both inside and outside the team—like blaming teammates when things went wrong and being too distracted by romantic relationships.

There wasn't any subject off-limits.

That's when I let them in on why my rules for who they could invite as dates were so strict.

"You guys that hunt, if you're gonna bag the biggest buck, where do you go to look for him?"

After a long silence and a couple of smart-aleck answers to ease the tension one of the boys said, almost mumbling, "I look for the doe."

"Bingo!" I snapped back. "You look for the doe! And it works that way in pretty much all of God's kingdom. So if I'm looking for a guy, where do you think I should start?"

"With the girls," they all answered in unison.

"That's right, I start with the girls. Guys, did you realize that the girls are part of this football team too?"

I saw a lot of eyebrows go up.

"Girls, whether you know it or not, you have a lot of influence over the choices these guys make. You can influence them positively or you can influence them negatively. Either way, you're going to have an impact on the success of the team."

"Let me give you an example. All of you girlfriends, let's say you're out with your boyfriend on a Thursday night. He knows he needs to go home early because he has a big game Friday night and needs a good night's sleep. But you're both still having fun. You're not ready to go home just yet. So you give him that little look—you know the one— where he instantly knows if he even thinks about going home, it will be a week before you speak to him again."

"So he doesn't get to bed until after midnight and he plays terribly on Friday night."

"Am I saying that's your fault? No! These guys are responsible for their own choices. But you can make things a lot easier on them by help- ing them, encouraging them, and supporting their commitment to the team. As a member of the team, you can have a positive impact on the team's success. And as the coach of this team, I really need your help getting this team on track."

I could see light bulbs going on all around the circle. It was beginning to make sense. The girls really seemed to like the idea of being part of the team.

In fact, one of them got so fired up she elbowed her boyfriend and said, "Yeah! It's not going to be my fault if you play bad and cause us to lose!"

I also spent a little time talking to the girls there who were not girl-friends—the ones who were already on a team representing our school. I reminded them that they had the same responsibility as the guys for making good choices, and that their choices would not only impact them as individuals and as teams, but also as a school. I told them they had the capacity to change the entire culture of the school if they wanted.

Then I asked all of them—boys and girls—if they had been making choices that they knew could hurt the team: Were they staying out late? Were they eating too much junk food? Were they cutting workouts short? Were they drinking? Were they hanging out with the wrong crowd?

Slips of Paper

I certainly had their attention then. They weren't used to thinking about things in that way. That's when I had them take out their slips of paper. I told them we were going to do a little exercise.

"I want you guys to write down anything you can think of—big or small—that you've done or said this season that's an excuse for not doing your best. Maybe you said something out loud to a friend, girl-friend, parent, or coach. Or maybe you didn't say anything at all, but you've thought about it—the excuse is just in your head."

The wide eyes I saw looking back at me told me I needed to give them a little reassurance.

"This is for you and you alone," I said. "I'm not going to take them up or grade them. No one's going to ask you what you wrote down. You are the only one that will ever lay eyes on that paper. When you're done writing, fold it so no one else can see what you've written."

I gave them about 10 minutes. While they worked, I stepped outside the circle and sat down so they wouldn't feel like I was looking over their shoulders.

The smoke rose into the dark of night that was almost as dark as the silence. The pop and crack of the fire was the only sound anyone heard. It was that intense kind of quiet—where you can almost hear the silence.

I remember while I was sitting there waiting, I looked over on the back porch and saw Colt and Chance playing quietly next to Debra (Case hadn't arrived yet). They weren't big enough to write, but they were sure giving it their best shot—scribbling in Crayon all over their pretend "excuse papers." They always loved doing anything the "big boys" did.

The guys were totally focused on their little white slips of paper in their hands. Toward the end of their time a few of them were still writing, but most of them just sat there and tried to stare a hole through the paper.

I knew some of the guys were really struggling. Excuses are never easy to admit. I should know—I've definitely had my share. Excuses are kind of like an escape hatch for life—a way out of doing things you really don't want to do. When you have to try and put those excuses on paper, it's like taking away the excuse's power to be an excuse anymore. It's a little scary. In fact, it's so scary; sometimes you just end up creating new excuses for why you can't write down any old excuses.

After everyone was done writing, I stepped back into the circle.

No More Excuses

"Y'all are sitting there holding in your hands all the excuses that you've used so far this season to keep you from being the best you can be," I said. "Now I want you to take a minute to look at these excuses and think about something."

"If you were to wake up tomorrow morning and all these excuses were gone—they just disappeared—what would your life look like? Think about how your life would be on the football field; how it would be at home; how it would be in the classroom. What would be different? What would you be able to accomplish?"

"More importantly, if all your excuses were gone tomorrow, who would it affect besides you? Your parents? Your friends? Your team? Your school?"

I could see it was becoming a real "aha" moment for some of them. I mean, it's one thing to think about things that hold you back. It's something completely different to imagine where you'd be if those things didn't hold you back.

"Okay. In just a minute, I'll ask you to bring your papers up here," which really heightened the anxiety.

I clarified, "But don't give them to me, just drop them in the fire. Yep, you're going to burn them up. Poof. You'll never have to use those excuses ever again, because they'll be gone—nothing but ashes."

But before we started throwing paper in the fire, I asked them to do one more thing.

"I want you guys to open up those papers right now and take a good look at them. I want you to read those excuses one more time before you throw them in the fire. Make sure you know everything that's on there. Commit it to memory. Because when the paper is gone, the excuses are gone too."

Then I asked them to come up and throw their papers in the fire.

I asked the seniors to come up first. They stood and gathered in a circle around the fire pit.

Some of their papers were folded in half; some had been folded in half so many times they almost disappeared.

Most of the guys had never done anything like this before. I could tell they weren't quite sure how to start. Were they supposed to do it all at one time? Were they supposed to do it one-by-one? They looked back and forth at each other, waiting for somebody to make the first move.

Finally, one of the guys stepped up and tossed his paper into the fire. The others quickly followed. After the seniors had their turn, I asked the rest of the group to come up—juniors next and then the sopho-mores (there weren't any freshmen on the team).

Some of them seemed a little self-conscious. They just kind of ran up to the fire, pitched the paper in, and then ran back to their seats. Some of them quickly tossed theirs in; others seemed really serious; some were even a little emotional. Then there were the guys who didn't really throw the paper in the fire so much as place it, and then stood there, staring at it until it turned to ashes and floated away.

All of them reacted a little differently to the whole experience, but the symbolism was still the same.

These guys were making a commitment—to me, to each other, and to themselves.

Family

The reason I put the whole party together was I thought it would help our athletes if we spent a little more time getting to know each other outside the locker room and off the football field—just hang out together and have some fun.

I'm also well acquainted with the reality that many high school boys live in. For a large number of boys, the closest thing they have to a father figure in their teenage years may be their coach. That puts an especially large burden on us coaches. We have such a short time in their forma-tive years to instill in them the values that will count for the rest of their lives. It really matters that we influence them in positive ways.

So many kids just don't have the kind of positive influence they need in their lives and the football field is one place they really get to shine. I started off telling the kids the excuses I used because I knew I needed to model leadership to them. I knew that many of the boys probably weren't going to see leadership modeled anywhere else. And I knew my coaches and I were only going to get so many chances with them.

I had made a commitment to do my very best for these guys.

More Than Football

But for me, it was about more than just becoming better football players. That's not to say it wasn't about football—it was. I mean, as their coach, it was my job to try and help them be better players.

But more than that, it was about changing bad habits and bad attitudes; about making good choices; about making them men of character and integrity.

I hoped that learning how to get rid of their excuses on the football field would better prepare them to get rid of bigger excuses later on— excuses for not being better men, better husbands, and better fathers.

Football is just a game. And like I said, there's very few high school football players that go on to the next level. But we as coaches have a tremendous opportunity to instill character into these boys. There's probably no one in a high school more aptly set up to teach these boys valuable life lessons than their coaches.

Hard work, discipline and teamwork are all things that are pivotal to the success of a football team (or any team). When we as coaches demand greatness from our players and they actually do them, we win football games. But the same things carry over into every aspect of a person's life. When we teach them not to give up and keep working harder and pressing themselves to do better, we're giving them the tools they need to succeed in life.

I wanted them to be winners at football, but more importantly, I wanted them to be winners at life.

How We Changed

We ended up really turning that football season around. After everyone had decided to give up their excuses and work hard as a team, we started playing up to the level of our talent. More importantly, we all, myself included, stopped using excuses the rest of that season. Our boys began taking responsibility for their own actions and their performance on the field was a "night-and-day" difference.

That evening had such a dramatic impact on our team that we didn't let it stop there. I made the campfire an annual event right before district play. I wanted to make sure we as a team were able to recalibrate just in time every year. Sometimes that's what it takes.

We have to make time to think about our excuses and then remove them from our circumstances. Only then can we focus on our own constraints and become better.

Only when we're willing to get rid of our excuses can we do our best—on and off the field.

Coach's Pep Talk
1. Fear drives most inappropriate behavior.
2. 99% of all failures are those that have perfected the art of making excuses.
3. The difference between Champs and Chumps is "U".

67

CHAPTER SIX

The Power of Traditions

As it turned out, Kenny, the young man who won the rock-throwing contest, was not the last boy to write his name on that rock. Another 19 names followed him.

We turned that team around so dramatically that I made sure we repeated the exercise of throwing our excuses in the fire year after year. And the rock-throwing contest had been such a hit, it all just naturally fit together. The whole thing became known as the "Rock Party."

It was a tradition that left an indelible mark on my athletes through the years as well as my own coaching career. There are lots of names scribbled on that rock—which now sits on my desk—that bring back memories from so many seasons. There were bad seasons that completely turned around after the rock party, and there were many good seasons that got much better.

Colt, Chance and Case had to wait for years to get to attend their first rock party as an athlete. They just couldn't wait to get to be one of the "big guys" chunking that rock across our field. But that's part of the point behind a good tradition, isn't it—to look forward to it.

I've had so many players come by my office through the years to look at that rock. Sometimes they've come back to town years after graduating just to look at the signatures on it and think about how that event changed that season, and influenced their lives. I always loved seeing my former athletes and coaches when they'd stop by to see the rock. I knew it symbolized something in their lives that made a difference.

It wasn't just my sons or the athletes that were changed by the rock party. Now that my coaching role has changed, my rock party days are over. But I've had several of my former assistant coaches from the years start their own rock parties. The tradition lives on through the lives of other coaches and players that may someday become coaches and teachers and leaders themselves.

Traditions Start Simply

I wasn't trying to start a tradition when I hosted that first rock party at my house. What I was trying to do was win a few football games and hopefully teach those kids some valuable lessons. I did put some thought and intentionality into what I was going to do and what I wanted everyone to get out of it, though, and that's really the birthplace of great traditions.

Traditions are not born out of accidents. When you put thought and energy into creating a moment it may just be the next thing that becomes a great tradition. Then again, it might not, but random activities almost never become traditions. At least not ones that shape things for the better.

To tell you the truth, I did a lot of things through the years that I put a lot of thought into, at home and as a coach, that didn't turn into traditions. Some other things did. The point is not trying to create a tradition, but making sure that what you do create is worthy of becoming one.

Thanksgiving

When my family first bought a ranch in the Texas Hill Country, it came with a bonus—its very own "cabin."

I have to put "cabin" in quotations because the thing wasn't entirely a cabin. It was actually one-half Airstream trailer and one-half dilapidated hunting shack. At some point somebody just stuck the two together and called it a cabin.

Not too long after we bought the place, we decided to do a little "redneck renovation." We started by removing the Airstream, and then we set about constructing the other half of the cabin. Let me be clear—this is definitely not something you'd see on a home renovation television show! There was nothing "extreme" about this makeover.

The original part of the cabin was like an old cowboy bunkroom with 8 or 10 metal bunk beds in it. I smile when I think about that creaking sound they made when someone would turn over. Since it already had sleeping quarters, when we added the other half, we made it into a small living area with a little kitchen about the size of a large closet, and a small bathroom with a shower.

Technically, we could take showers. All the right equipment was there. But, because the water came from an old cistern attached to a windmill on the property, if the wind wasn't blowing, we were kind of out of luck. If we wanted to get clean, we had to wait until a nice breeze blew up.

There was electricity in the cabin, but no phones. This was the late 1980's, so most people's phones were still attached to walls. So we were kind of on our own out there in the middle of nowhere. If anyone needed to communicate with the outside world, we had to make a long drive into town.

There was a small TV in the cabin, but obviously no cable. And the "rabbit ears" didn't help much. The channels were mostly just snow, so about the only thing we used the TV for was to watch videotapes we'd brought from home.

The cabin was furnished with hand-me-downs from family members—an old sleeper sofa of my grandmother's; a nightstand from my Mom and Dad's house; a chair that had belonged to Debra's parents. It was quite a collection. The "décor" was kind of like the furniture. A lot of it was hand-me-downs. But we also had stuff gathered from around the property; flowers, branches, and colorful leaves that were made into artistic arrangements (my Mom was really good at that).

That was our cabin. And we loved it. A tiny little ramshackle place in the middle of the ruggedly beautiful Texas Hill Country, surrounded by rolling hills dotted with limestone and granite, and big patches of oak, cedar, and mesquite trees.

This is the place where myself, Debra, the kids and my entire extended family—9 adults and 7 kids—have spent Thanksgiving every year for almost 20 years.

Our Cabin Overfloweth

I know. It sounds kind of crazy. I guess the idea of spending three or four days with 15 of your closest relatives in a 1200-square-foot shack isn't everybody's idea of fun. But it was for us, mostly because we were blessed with a family that enjoyed spending time together.

My father, Burl McCoy or "Daddy Burl" as he was known to the grand-kids, was a great source of traditions at those gatherings. He's always been so intentional about the things he's done with the family, and he's also produced some of our best light-hearted traditions. He's one of those men who don't know the meaning of slowing down, and through the years he never has.

It doesn't seem to matter where we are, but anytime our family is together more than 12 hours my father will come into the family room and ask if anyone wants to go pick up rocks to clear a field. Early on even Debra got snookered into it once or twice, but now she, like everyone else, knows better. Colt, Chance and Case seem to know when he's about to ask and they make themselves scarce. The tradition isn't actually picking up rocks (which no one does anymore) but that we know dad's going to ask. It just wouldn't be a family gathering anymore if he didn't. We all smile and snicker and say something like, "that's Dad." Everyone's picked up enough rocks over the years to know he's actually serious, but I know he likes the reaction he gets now when he asks.

Dad's traditions aren't just related to piling up an infinite number of Texas hill country rocks, though. His are some of the most memorable of the McCoy clan. Whenever we have gotten together as a family dad has always taken time to sit down with the children and teach them. It's probably a little of the coach in him, but he's never comfortable with leaving a family gathering without having been intentional to pour some of his life into the next generations. Dad's been able to teach the kids so many valuable lessons that he's learned from his years of wisdom and I'm still learning from him myself.

That's something that we all hold dear about my father and I think its something that's missing from many families nowadays. Whether the younger generations simply just don't listen to their elders or older generations have become suspiciously quiet, there doesn't seem to be much cross-generational communication anymore. Some families are just too broken to give anyone the opportunity to learn from grand-parents, but it's too important to miss out on. Daddy Burl isn't just my boys' grandfather who shows up at family gatherings and loves on the kids. He's someone they love and respect immensely. They value and seek his advice and counsel for many things in life to this day, as do I.

Dad's made a tradition out of sitting the grandkids down and talking to them, but it's not simply talking to them that's so valuable to all of us; he's intentional about teaching important things. He's never wanted to miss an opportunity to impart character, values and integrity to his family, and it just wouldn't feel right to leave a Thanksgiving or any other gathering without it.

That's one thing about traditions--even if they're good they can still be squandered. After one event sticks and becomes a tradition it still takes effort to make sure that subsequent events are as meaningful as the one that started it. That doesn't necessarily mean that you have to put a lot of work into things. It doesn't require any planning for my father to holler for all the kids to come into the room and listen to him, but he's intentional about doing it every time we gather. I know it could be so easy to get full of Thanksgiving turkey and just want to relax and skip "Daddy Burl teaching time," but most of the effort is really just remembering to yell at the kids to come into the room.

Lasting Positive Impacts

It may be an exaggeration to say that my father never misses an opportunity at a family gathering to teach the kids, but if he's missed one it doesn't stand out in my mind. The real point is that it's such a valuable tradition to us that it would seem a travesty to lose it. That's another power of traditions—the positive impact they leave on us.

All traditions will probably leave an impact, but not all of them are good. If your favorite family tradition is sitting around after Christmas dinner to wait for uncle Charlie to get drunk and say stupid things I'd recommend replacing it with something more valuable. Does everyone at your gatherings end up just watching television and not engage with each other? Try turning the television off for 30 minutes and telling each other what they mean to you. If that's too sappy for you, just spend time talking about your favorite family moments of the past year.

If you're a boss, don't let your annual golf tournament be your only tradition. That probably doesn't leave an impact on anyone other than they know it will happen. It doesn't have to be something corny, but build into your culture something that inspires people. It was always remarkable to see how our team's morale changed after the rock party. Throwing excuses into a fire may be a little much for the workplace, but there are plenty of intentional things you could do well in an office environment to make lasting impacts on people.

Creating events that are worthy of traditions is the place to start. Our family cabin wasn't the tradition itself; it was just the environment that great traditions grew out of. The tradition was Thanksgiving, which isn't a McCoy tradition; it's an American tradition. The McCoy traditions were fostered by an environment that forced us into making them. We didn't rely on the television much for entertainment, so we had to come up with things to do. Many of those things we did early on are what turned into great traditions and have had lasting impacts on all of us.

It's important to create that environment—no matter if it's your home, your workplace or your team—it's what leads to so many great traditions.

Thanksgiving Before Sunup

A big part of our tradition at the cabin came very early on Thanksgiving morning.

A couple of hours before the sun came up, all the guys (except for the littlest ones) would slip out of bed, pull on a few layers of clothes, gather up all their gear, and set out with flashlights into the bitterly cold pre-dawn darkness.

The darkness was always so thick it seemed like it would almost swallow us—the kind of darkness you can only experience when you're far away from a big halo of city lights.

When Colt, Chance, and Case were younger, they were always a little spooked to be out in the woods in the dark, so they usually stuck pretty close by, especially when we veered off the gravel road into the thick grass and cover of oak trees. I would always be leading the way with the flashlight while the boys tried to walk exactly in my footsteps.

For the first little bit, nobody talked. The only sound we heard was the sound of leaves and gravel crunching under our shoes. But at some point, the boys would inevitably start making noise—talking, laughing, or just generally cutting up. So I'd have to turn around, press my index finger against my lips, and give them the universal "shhhh" sign. After all, the whole object of the exercise was to be as quiet as possible.

Then, for a few minutes, they'd try extra hard not to make a sound— walking slowly heel-to-toe over the dry grass and brush. But that usually didn't last long. Suddenly, I'd hear the sharp crack of a dry branch or the loud clack of rocks behind me. It was still too dark to see any wildlife around us, but I could imagine everything scattering for several miles.

Sometimes we heard movement in the darkness. I always tried to kind of play it up a little bit because the boys always got so fired-up. I'd usually stop suddenly and hold my hand out to the side with my open palm facing them, signaling them to stop. Then I'd hold my index finger in front of my lips, cock my ear in the direction of the sound, squint my eyes, and scan the darkness for movement.

The boys were always wide-eyed and they were usually locked on me. I guess they were waiting for some indication that maybe it was time for us to run.

But we never had to. More often than not, the sound was coming from some kind of varmint, like an armadillo, who can make a huge racket when rooting around for grubs under a carpet of dry leaves.

Once I spotted the hunting blind, I would shine the light on it so the boys could see where we were headed. Sometimes the blinds were on the ground; sometimes they were on a top of a metal scaffold, or in a tree. They weren't always easy to find in the darkness, but the shape of a 5-by-5 box usually stands out against the background of uneven shapes in the woods. When I shined the light directly on it, it just looked like a big box with dark, narrow slits for windows.

Getting into a dark blind is a trick in itself, especially if it was the first time that season that we'd been out there. It was always a little spooky, even for me. Hunting blinds are pretty popular places for all kinds of critters seeking shelter. There was always the possibility when I opened the door that I would run into some kind of wildlife I hadn't expected—a snake maybe, or a raccoon. In fact, one year, Colt and I had a little wrestling match with a barn owl that was just as surprised to see us as we were to see him.

While the objective was always to be as quiet as possible, after we started climbing into the blind, that usually became a moot point. Everybody had to bang and rattle around a while to get their gear in place and get situated. And of course, whoever ended up with the creaky chair or stool had to quickly figure out some way to keep it quiet.

So there was always some amount of noise. But if we got out early enough and got quiet pretty quick, we could still have a good hunt.

For me, it wasn't really about the hunt anyway. It was about sitting there with my sons in the dark silence, peering out the narrow windows, anxiously waiting for the world to wake up.

When night finally turned to day, it was almost imperceptible. One minute we'd be staring out into the darkness, and the next minute, we'd begin to see the landscape emerge in colorless grey shapes. Then, little by little, the light began to fill in the shapes with colors.

It was about that time that the wildlife began to wake up. It usually started with a few birds. Then, within a matter of just a few minutes, it was like a million other birds had joined in the chorus. It almost seemed deafening after the long silence.

The boys and I would sit as still as possible—like little statues, letting out little puffs of warm breath into the cold November air—trying not to make any sudden movements that might scare the wildlife. We scanned the landscape looking for deer, wild turkey, or even wild hogs.

Every now and again, one of the boys would whisper something or ask a question. Sometimes I would answer and then it would get quiet again. Or, sometimes, we'd get so busy talking and laughing that we'd just forget about the hunt—probably not a bad thing since we'd probably scared off everything within a hundred miles.

But it didn't really matter. We were together and we were having fun.

Of course, the boys could only take sitting still so long before their stomachs started making hunger noises. We'd usually head back to the cabin around 9:30. By this time, all the ladies were up with the little ones who were too young to go with us. They'd usually have a huge breakfast—bacon, eggs, sausage, and biscuits—waiting for us when we got back.

After breakfast, the kids would usually go out and play for a while. They would go hiking, exploring, fishing in the creek, climbing on hay bales, you name it. But there was more to the ranch than fun and games, because it was an operational ranch. My Dad often put the older kids to work feeding cattle, mending fences, and doing other ranch-related chores (like picking up rocks). It would end up being a pretty full morning.

Making Memories

I don't have little boys anymore. If Colt, Chance or Case want to go hunting now, they don't necessarily need me. Looking back on those times is pure pleasure to their father's heart. I love thinking about the times we spent in those spider-infested shacks we called hunting blinds. I love to think back on how big those little boys' eyes would get when they thought they heard some critter milling around in the dry leaves near them.

We can't ever go back to recreate the moments of the past, so making sure that we make the most of the moments we have now is important. The events that I create now have the chance to be the lasting beautiful memories in my future, so it's critical to make sure they have every opportunity to be good ones.

Our cabin felt like insanity sometimes with all the people in it, but when Debra and I felt a little overwhelmed we'd always say to each other, "Remember, we're busy making memories!"

We didn't just hope that the things we did would be great memories in the future, we made sure they were worthy of them. I don't want to make it sound like every single thing we did was with an eye on the future. We didn't constantly question ourselves with, "is this something that's going to be a great memory someday?" What we did do, though, was stop doing things that we knew weren't the stuff of good memories. What I mean is that it doesn't take a database and a computer analyst trying to figure out if everything you do is tradition-worthy, it just takes a small amount of intentionality and ingenuity.

When I put together activities for my football team I always made sure they aligned with the values and character I was trying to instill in the boys. Was it going to teach them how to be better football players and men? If not, I didn't do it. If for some reason I did do something that failed that test, I always made sure I never did it again. And I had a lot of fails over the years that needed correction.

Leaving Legacies

The busted plans we make shouldn't keep us from continuing to try for the future. Great traditions like the rock party were worth the many other failures I had along the way. The greatest power of things like the rock party is not that I was able to change a few boys' lives here and there, but that it was actually valuable enough to so many people that it's left a legacy now.

Traditions have the greatest power to leave a legacy than almost anything else we do. My father's times in front of the fire with the grandkids at the cabin or at other gatherings aren't just great stories now—they've left him a legacy with his descendants. We're more connected to him in ways that will live beyond his years. And mine.

My father has left a lasting legacy with all the things he's been to our family. So many of the things that I think and do I got directly from him. The funny thing is, most of them I don't remember—I don't find out they're actually from my dad until I do them and my mother or Debra points it out. The things I do remember, the things I'm sure are from my Dad, are the things that I remember from our great family traditions of years past.

I hope to leave a legacy with all the important people in my life—my family, my football teams, and my coworkers. I'm sure that some of the things I've done with people that aren't associated with traditions through the years may have had an impact, but I know it's the things that happened year after year and season after season that leave the biggest impact on our minds.

After Debra and I are long gone, will our kids continue to do the things together as a family we've done for years? Will there be football teams out there that have some version of their own rock party? If the answer is yes, then we can rest someday as happy people because we'll have left a worthy legacy—the real power of traditions.

Coach's Pep Talk
1.   Most people know what to do; few people do what they know.
2.   Remember the banana—when he left the bunch, he got skinned.
3.   Go the extra mile; it's never crowded.
4.   Think big, believe big, act big and the results will be big.

CHAPTER SEVEN

Perseverance

The 2007 season had hit an all-time low. We'd only won 2 games and lost 4, and we hadn't even started district play. Things just weren't looking good. To make matters worse, it was Chance's senior season and he was really frustrated by how things were going.

It's definitely hard on us when things don't go our way when our expectations are high.

We were in Wichita Falls playing a tough game. We weren't playing as well as I knew we could and we were committing penalties that were really killing us. The final blow came when Chance was interfered with on a pass in the end zone and the flag never came. He ran over to the referee, and although he didn't really say anything, his body language said it all. Let's just say that it was enough to draw a personal foul from Chance.

Before the penalty we were still in good shape to possibly score and win the game. After the penalty we got pushed back far enough that the new yardage was insurmountable with so little time left. We ended up losing the game, not just because of Chance's behavior, but because of lots of penalties and bad performance.

We're A Team

The personal fouls were unacceptable, though. I knew it and Chance knew it. I sent everyone except Chance and Heath (the other boy who'd committed personal fouls that night—I think they had 4 between them) to the locker room without saying much else. Heath was a senior leader I had great respect for but he had also lost control of his emotions during the game much like Chance.

Chance knew that around the McCoy household we don't wait around to correct bad behavior. We take care of it right then and there. I told Chance and Heath that their behavior was unacceptable. It hurt the team, and they were going to pay a price, that night. Their actions and behaviors were seen in public, so the consequence would be too—they were going to have to run "over-backs" on the field. Over-backs are when we sprint from one sideline to the other and back, twice. Chance looked at me and said, "Yes sir. I deserve it tonight. I know I messed up."

Neither boy was upset about having to run that night because they knew that's how we dealt with problems on the field. I wasn't out to embarrass them so I made them do it on the darker end of the field, but there were still a lot of fans left in the stadium.

I'm not the kind of coach that's about making the boys run when their in trouble "until *I* get tired," but they were going to run more than a couple of these. If you've ever run anything like over-backs then you know they can sting, especially after a long football game.

After the two had done one set of over-backs we heard the distinct clanking of football pads in swift motion. I turned to see the commotion of almost the entire team coming back onto the field, led by our freshman quarterback, Case.

"Coach, we're a team, and if one of us is gonna run, we're all gonna run!" one of the seniors yelled as they ran up to us.

All the rest of them chimed in agreement. I looked at them, thought for a moment about it, and said, "Okay, you'll all run then."

I made them all do a couple more over-backs and told them to go to the locker room. I hadn't noticed that the people in the stands were definitely taking notice of what was going on by then. What *they* hadn't noticed was that the two boys had started out by themselves. The fans and parents didn't know that when the rest of the team got back to the locker room they realized Chance and Heath weren't there and saw them on the field running. All but a handful of boys immediately ran back out on the field to run with them by their own choice.

When I got to the edge of the field to go into the locker room I was met with some less than friendly parents. I heard statements like, "Can't coach 'em, so you're gonna make 'em run, huh McCoy?"

"Gonna punish all our boys for your bad coaching?" another said.

"You're just trying to embarrass our kids for losing!" from still another.

Some of them just glared at me and nodded their heads in agreement as we made our way through the crowd from the field to the locker room.

The parents were hot because to them it looked like I was the irate coach who was taking our failure out on a bunch of little high school kids. Nothing could've been further from the truth. In fact, I used to actually run with the boys when I'd have them do over-backs for reminders of our expectations. I stopped that as I got older, not because I'm too out of shape to do them, but because it was only proving to my own pride that I could still do them—the boys didn't learn anything from me burning *my* lungs out.

I left the field house late that night knowing that many parents just didn't understand what had happened. My only hope was that their boys were going to explain to them what happened and that they'd be reasonable enough to listen. But it's never easy on a coach to lose a big game and have part of your parental support wondering if you should even be the coach in charge of their kids—let alone the whole athletic program.

To make matters worse, five of my kids went to a party the next night and got crazy and broke some of our team rules. Ironically, three of the boys who got in trouble were the ones who stayed back in the locker room when the team came back on the field the night before to run with Chance and Heath.

When I say they broke our team rules, I'm talking about a code of conduct that our school had in place for teams or individuals that competed outside of the school day. It generally included things like drug, alcohol and tobacco use. Some years we would go further and create a "Social Contract" with our teams that spelled out how we wanted to be treated and how we want to treat our teammates and coaches, along with many other social issues such as a curfew, language, and the consequences associated with breaking those rules.

When those five boys came to practice on Monday, it was obvious through their sluggishness and chatter that they'd broken the rules. Everyone on the team knew it including me, so I sat them down after practice and they had no problem confessing to their involvement. I told them they were going to go through the discipline outlined in our social contract—that they would sit out for two games—punishment they knew they would suffer before they went out partying that night. Before I even finished they all told me that it wasn't that important to them anymore and they were quitting the team.

Making Something Great

I've got to say that anytime a kid quits my team, I take it personally. I feel it's a failure on my part to properly motivate that athlete to want to play for our team. Having five of them quit at once really stung, and it took me a few weeks to really get over it.

The pressure from parents and school administration was hard to take over the next few days, but we dealt with it and kept on doing the things I knew would give our team a shot. I had great support from my friend and Superintendent, Dr. Beau Rees, who gave me confidence that I was doing the right thing. The practices really started to come together those next few days. Running those over-backs together after the game that night had really proven to be a bonding experience for our team.

In addition, our team chemistry and unity seemed to be a lot better. I don't know if it was because some had left the team or our leaders finally decided to step up. Whatever the reason, the team started to gel and play up to their potential. We won the remaining district games, where we were big underdogs, finished with a record of 5-5 and won the District Championship. We went on to win Bi-District and Area Championships and eventually were knocked out of the playoffs in the third round.

A team that underperformed most of the season took advantage of a negative event and persevered through some tough times. They changed the way they wanted to be remembered and ended up playing football in December.

The team's perseverance really paid off that season. To think, it was an error in judgment on Chance's part that started the chain of events that led to a transformation. He and all of us persevered through some tough times and in the end we built something very special.

It was only a period of a few days, but I was under pretty intense pressure to apologize to parents for making their kids run. No one actually asked me to, but I understood their outrage from the events on the field that night. I knew I had to stand my ground, but the pressure was still there. And it really helped having a superintendent who stood behind me. That's invaluable—having people, even if they're few and far between—who will stand with you in times where you need help to persevere.

Our team certainly stood with one another to persevere through that season, and they made something great out of it.

Starting From Scratch

Chance had been a good athlete from a very early age, and even in junior high he was a really great quarterback. When he joined my team, Colt was the senior quarterback and what we really needed was another wide receiver. I asked him if he'd make the switch and he gladly agreed. He became one of Colt's favorite targets that year and because of it was named to the all-state team as a wide receiver.

When Colt graduated I asked Chance if he wanted to try and move back to quarterback, but he refused because he'd grown to really love receiving. He didn't feel the need to follow in Colt's footsteps just to prove he could be as good a quarterback (a comparison that Chance has heard many times). He was his own guy and he'd really found what he enjoyed.

I'd been the head coach for a number of years at Jim Ned High School when I realized that some of the things I wanted to do to further our program weren't really on the school board's agenda. I got along well with most of the school board and I really liked my Superintendent, Kent LeFever, but the board and I no longer saw eye to eye on the direction of the program. After a lot of thought I knew it was time for me to step aside and let someone else be a voice for them to take the program to another level.

The decision was made pretty easy for me because another school had been calling me about their athletic director and coaching position. They were going to give me the freedom to do all the things that I wanted to do where I currently was. It was the right time to go.

We made the move during the spring of Chance's sophomore year. That was hard on Chance because we were leaving a culture that was used to winning and something he was comfortable with to a team culture that hadn't won a playoff game in 11 years.

Chance was a leader; so having to regain that leadership role at a new school was difficult for him, especially since he was only a sophomore. It's never easy for anyone, but he was following in some big footsteps. Colt had gone on to the University of Texas and had been talked up as their next starting quarterback, so there was a lot of pressure from the other students for Chance to be a great quarterback for them. When they found out Chance wasn't going to play quarterback they started letting him have it.

"You're no Colt," they'd say. "We thought you could be as good as your brother."

Chance took it all in stride and determined he was going to show them all he was a great athlete in his own right. He was going to prove to them on the field that he was his own guy and he didn't have to answer to comparisons between he and his brother. He worked hard to show everyone, including himself, it was true.

He did just that. He went on to make the all-state team his junior and senior years in football. He was also an All District basketball player and competed for the Pole Vault championship and placed 3rd his senior year.

Chance was a tremendous all-around athlete. He had suffered from some speed and agility setbacks because in junior high he'd broken his leg on a growth plate. That had really stunted him, but he kept on pushing himself and it paid off. He never let anything keep him from achieving his goals.

But things didn't come easy for Chance. When it was time for college, he had a few Division 1 schools recruit him, but when it came time to make a decision, none of them panned out. He decided to accept a scholarship from my alma mater, Abilene Christian University, a Division 2 school. His playing career is over after a rocky 4 years that ended with a great season at Hardin Simmons University, where he started at receiver for the Cowboys' nationally ranked football team.

Chance has persevered through everything life has thrown at him, and he's done it well.

I'm proud of all three of my sons, but I've loved watching Chance as he's handled difficult circumstances. We all have bad circumstances that come up in life. How we handle those circumstances reveals what we're made of on the inside. Do we fold under the pressure of difficult circumstances, or do we rise to the occasion and put in whatever work it takes to overcome them?

Chance pushed through tough circumstances in the past and he continues to do it today. He, as well as Case and Colt, worked hard to persevere through the things that would have held them back—not the least of which being the moves to new towns and having to start over every few years.

My Career

Life in a coaching family can be hard. You may think that only professional football coaches get fired when their teams have a bad season, but the truth is it happens all the way down the chain. I used to hear from those who were older and wiser than me that "you're not a real Texas football coach until you've been fired." I always thought they were just blowing smoke. 27 years of coaching later I understand.

I graduated from Abilene Christian University and went on staff as a quarterback and receiver coach. It was a great opportunity right out of the gate, but when Debra and I got married we thought it would be fun to try a job out of state, so I took a position as the offensive coordinator in Lovington, New Mexico.

Lovington was a great program and we loved it there. I really grew as a coach and learned a lot more about the game. We won two state championships in my time there, but after five years Debra and I felt it was time to move back a little closer to home. We had a budding little family now, and let's face it, there's nothing like Texas football!

I took a coordinator's position in San Saba, Texas with an old college teammate, Hal Wason. Hal stuck around another year and was ready to move, so when he packed his bags I got the job. It was my first head-coaching job and I was ready to cut my teeth. It was definitely a steep learning curve, but I felt like I found my place as a head coach. I loved it there, but as we coaches often do, I got itchy feet for something a little bigger, so we uprooted after 6 years and four playoff berths.

We moved to Kermit, Texas and realized almost immediately we'd made a mistake. Kermit is still in Texas, but it's actually the same distance away from our family in Abilene as Lovington was. We loved the town of Kermit, the school and the football program, but we just knew that we were too far away from family. We weren't happy there and we had to make the hard decision to leave after one year.

I hated to do that to the athletes on my team there, but when you find yourself in one of those situations; it's much better in the long run, for everyone, to make the right move as soon as possible. We could have stayed there another two or three years, but everyone would have suffered from my family's misery.

We moved from Kermit to Hamlin, Texas where I became the athletic director. From Hamlin we moved to Tuscola, Texas to Jim Ned High School.

As you can imagine, every move was filled with new opportunities and broken hearts as we left behind great friends, but Debra, Colt, Chance and Case were always troopers when we moved. We'd shed our tears over leaving good friends behind and prepare ourselves for our next challenge.

Moving a lot requires a lot of perseverance on the part of a family. It can be easy to move to a new location and decide to give up on making friends. It's really hard to leave old friends behind and a lot of work to make new ones. That kind of attitude only leads to isolation, and isolation can destroy a person. It will rob you of so many things and take your eyes off the goals you had in life that caused you to make a move in the first place.

Honestly, our family didn't struggle too much with isolation from our moves, but we still had to be diligent and intentional about making new friends after each move.

Fortunately we found great people that we still love to this day in every place we moved. There were, of course, rough spots along the way...

Coaching Football in Texas

Television shows like Friday Night Lights may make Texas football a little overdramatized, but there's no denying that football is king on Friday nights in the Lone Star State. And that really shows when it comes to your coaching job.

You can be riding high on the praises of everyone in a small Texas town one day and the next find your head on the "chopping block". People are fickle when it comes to sports and football is serious business in these small towns. The old saying of "what have you done for me *lately?*" is the mantra in high school football.

Stories like the ire of parents after making boys run was not an isolated incident. We had lots of things happen like that over the years, but most of them were mostly anonymous.

Suffering the abuse of anonymous boosters was especially hard when the kids were young, though. They just didn't understand why people would do what they'd do. There were so many times after a difficult loss we'd wake up on Saturday or Sunday mornings to find suitcases or for sale signs littering our yards. The "better pack your bags" symbolism was never lost on us, but Debra and I knew people just do silly things like that. The boys really couldn't understand why people wouldn't like Daddy.

I got into the car for the drive home from one tough game when the kids were young and noticed everyone was still a little sniffly and teary-eyed. Unfortunately that night Debra and the boys were sitting in front of a man who wasn't afraid to share his opinions out loud and in colorful ways about what he thought of coach McCoy.

Those kinds of things are probably harder on a coach's family than they are on a coach himself. As a coach, you learn to block out such mean-spirited criticism like that. And since I grew up in a family where my father was a coach, I knew what I was getting into. The kids and Debra eventually learned to deal with it and years later when we pulled up to our house to find for sale signs and road blocks in our driveway, we'd just laugh about it.

It took a lot of growing for the boys, especially, but we all learned to take it in stride. There were some places that were better than others about things like that, but it can really teach you a lot about shutting out the negative voices. To persevere through challenging times, especially when those challenges are created by nay-sayers, it's critical to be able to shut out the voices of those who'd prefer to see you fail.

We've Got A Lot Of Work To Do

Learning to persevere through the difficulties of a move is challenging, even for the gregarious McCoys. Managing expectations about what the new life will be like and overcoming the setbacks from our expectations are great learning lessons for kids and parents alike.

Chance had been a high performer and an excellent leader at the school we were at. When we moved to Graham, Texas, he had to start all over again. The character and integrity he'd worked hard to build in himself were challenged almost immediately.

Chance was a sophomore and he had an 11pm curfew on weekend nights (not the team's social contract, but Mom and Dad's). Not long after getting to school and making a few friends he went out on a Saturday night. We didn't expect to see him until around his curfew, so we made plans to go out on the town ourselves. We showed back up at the house around 9:30 to find Chance already home. Debra and I were surprised.

"What are you doing home so early, Chance?" Debra asked.

Looking at me he said, "We've got a lot of work to do, Dad."

That was all he needed to say. We understood exactly what had happened and why he was home. Whatever plans the guys Chance was out with had somehow denigrated into activities that he wasn't okay with. And most of these guys were on the football team!

Chance later told us that standing up for what he believed was an uphill battle there. He knows that drinking, smoking and drugs are off-limits, but he's always been good at standing up for himself and knowing why. He'd often have to argue his case that those things weren't good for their bodies and they weren't going to be able to perform as well on the field. Then there were the times he had to play the "that's just wrong" card. And when all that didn't work, Chance would remove himself from the situation entirely. He wasn't going to be a party to anything that went against his own code of conduct.

And he was really good about holding that line in high school.

Chance would find that standing up and keeping his values and standards high was even more of an uphill battle once he got to college than it was in high school. With a college career that was full of more downs than ups, Chance was challenged in many ways to persevere through the times in his life where things just didn't go like he dreamed they would.

But Chance never quits.

When It's Okay To Quit

Quitting has never been an option at the McCoy household. From our football games out in the yard when the boys were young to playing for a national championship, we've just never let it into our vernacular. But is it ever okay to quit?

One of the schools I coached at, which will remain nameless here, I had to leave after a little battle with the school board. I hold high standards for our athletes (and I've never made excuses for that). Every one of my football teams has had a code of conduct to live up to. The expectations were always known as well as the consequences

But holding people to high standards sometimes crosses people's lines. I got called in to meet with the school board at this school to discuss my contract renewal. We'd had a particularly good season, so I thought things were going to go fairly well with them.

They listed off the accomplishments the program had gone through while I'd been there and thanked me for my hard work. Then they told me I was too hard on the kids and that if I didn't agree to back off they weren't going to renew my contract. I was a little puzzled so I tried to dialogue with them a little bit about what they meant.

Our team's "social contract" involved things outside the realm of football and they didn't like that. It turns out that several of the board members didn't think it was any of my business to know what the kids did after they left my practices or games, especially on the weekends. They felt like my jurisdiction ended at the football field. My mandate from them was back off or get fired.

I told them that there was no way I was backing down on my convictions about how to coach kids and the expectations I held for them. What the boys did on Saturday night absolutely affected how they played the next week. It also affected who they would become when they grew up, which I was infinitely more concerned with. Were they going to be men of character and integrity, and more importantly, was I going to be a man in their life who held them to high standards?

The board and I absolutely did not see eye to eye. They may have had a good reason to feel the way they did, but I couldn't see it. I knew we weren't going to come to terms. But I asked them to cut me a deal. I said if they'd renew my contract I'd spare them the trouble it causes when they cancel a contract and I'd have a new job in six weeks. They were very gracious to agree. And I had a new job in three weeks.

And so the McCoy family was on the road yet again, off to experience a new town with new faces and challenges.

What Perseverance Looks Like

That doesn't mean it wasn't difficult on my family and I. We were comfortable where we were and we really liked things. We had good friends, a good church and a nice life. There was of course the temptation to pander to someone else's values, but I knew I just couldn't, no matter what it cost me. Really, if you do cave in on your values, you never gain anything. So at that point, there was nowhere to go but down if I stayed.

Persevering through difficult breaks like that looks like having to tell your family that we're moving again when the day before they thought everything was fine. Looking them in the eyes and seeing the pain of "oh no, we've really got to move again?" sure makes you think about wavering on your values. It's hard, but you do it because it's the right thing to do.

And it all comes down to that; are you willing to do the right thing no matter what? Not to say that I always did what was right, because I didn't, but we must always try to live to that standard.

Perseverance takes so many forms through your life. Fighting to gain acceptance in a new place and sticking to your values like Chance did showed a lot of courage. It's a scenario he's been through a few times and I'm sure he'll go through it again.

Perseverance looks like making the tough decision to move away from a great place because it's the right thing to do. Perseverance also looks like a family sticking together through thick and thin as they pack up and move to new town after new town and do it with joy.

In the end, the temptation to quit to make life easier never has nearly as good a payoff as the will to persevere.

Coach's Pep Talk

1. The one who says it cannot be done is generally passed up by someone doing it.
2. Hard work beats talent when talent doesn't work hard.
3. There are four reasons for failure: 1) A Lust for laziness, 2) A want to be popular rather than respected, 3) A fear of failure and 4) No obligation to responsibility.

CHAPTER EIGHT

Consequences and Tough Decisions

Colt looked at me with anticipation as he, Chance and I walked out of the locker room at half time.

"Are you going to play them, Dad?" he asked

"You know I'm not." I said.

Colt looked at Chance and said, "That's Dad."

It was as if he already knew the answer but he felt he ought to ask me anyway.

Colt and Chance both had bye weeks at college, so they were able to come home for one game during their brother's senior season. And since Colt had a bye week, ESPN thought it would be a good idea to get that "where he came from" story and sent their big mobile studio that night to film Graham High School's game against Bridgeport.

To add to the drama, we were 4-0 and ranked in the top 10 (as was our opponent) and we looked like we had a great chance for a good playoff run. That's why suspending 5 of our starters had upset parents, confused the media and caused the rest of our small town team to play some good old iron-man football.

Why were they suspended? For breaking the rules, of course.

As part of the curfew rule for the team everyone had to be home by 10pm on weeknights and midnight on Saturdays. No exceptions. I mean, they're teenage boys, so nothing good is going to happen after midnight on Saturday, anyway.

Seven of our boys had broken curfew and been at a party where they should not have been on the previous Saturday night. They hadn't violated any of the major code of conduct rules, but they had enjoyed way too much of the morning hours. On Monday, the whole team seemed to really be dragging. I knew something was up, but I didn't bring it up. After practice, several of the guys came to me and apologized for the bad practice we'd had. They confessed to the Saturday night escapades and they knew it was their fault the whole team dragged that afternoon.

I told them I appreciated their honesty and that none of them would play during the next game. The look of shock on their faces removed the need for words. "Certainly he's not serious?" I could hear their thoughts. I saw it in their eyes.

We had a rule, and I wasn't about to budge. I ran the whole situation past my superintendent, Dr. Reese. He seemed to think that the punishment was a little harsh, given the fact that the boys hadn't broken the school code of conduct policy—just the "social contract" we had with our team—but he supported my decision and respected my position as the coach.

The dynamics from the town really were something. The range of mad, sad and glad was almost overwhelming. I had parents who were upset that their son wasn't going to be playing because it might hurt their chances of playing in college. I had teachers who were disappointed that the punishment was so severe, and some that thought it wasn't severe enough. And I had some parents who were happy I did it. They were just glad some of these boys had actually been told "no" for once in their lives. I'd have to say that overall everyone was supportive of the decision.

It didn't matter what anyone's reaction was; I was holding my ground. Not because I wanted to make an example out of these boys. These were good boys and I loved every one of them. It was hard on me to bench them. It hurt me, and I was a good friend to some of their parents and I knew how much it was hurting them, but I was committed to growing our team no matter the outcome. I knew that even if we lost the game, our season would be better for it. And not only our season, but all the boys' lives on the team for seeing that there were consequences for their actions, and a "big game" didn't change that.

I wasn't trying to make an example of the 7 boys who broke curfew, but I was trying to nip something in the bud. If you waver the first time someone crosses the line you've set, you'll be fighting bigger battles for months, and then where do you decide to draw the line? Who knows, maybe if we let this one go, the next time drugs would be involved?

The Second Half

Those boys came out of the locker room at half time really thinking they were going to play. The look on their eyes as we came back on the field said, "You're going to put us back in now, right coach?" Before the game I told them to suit up, but they were going to be on the sidelines cheering and encouraging more than anyone else in the stadium. When I reiterated that as we came back on the field, I could see their hopes dashed, but they sucked it up and hooted and hollered all the more. I was really proud of them.

That game was tough, though. The previous year we lost to Bridgeport 59-27. They had rolled to 478 yards of total offense without any turnovers and we only scored once in the second half. We had a much better team this year, but when the Bridgeport boys found out about the suspensions, they thought they had our number.

There were multiple personal fouls (roughing the quarterback) against Case in the first half. We started out behind, so being down at half time by only 7 points didn't seem so bad except we had several guys playing on both sides of the ball.

Our boys were worn out, but they kept fighting through the second half. At the start of the 4th quarter we were still down 7 points. As both teams were wearing out, we tied the game. Our boys on defense held the Bridgeport boys to a quick series and we got the ball back with a few minutes left.

We caught our break when we drove 80 yards for the go ahead touchdown. It was a moment where everyone thought they could breathe a sigh of relief.

Unfortunately, our defense let down their guard a little too much and Bridgeport came back with a quick score with only a few seconds left on the clock. That put them only one point down with their field goal team coming onto the field for the extra point. Our team was devastated.

That's when our middle linebacker, Ethan Hiser stepped up. Ethan had been playing on both sides of the ball to cover for one of the suspended boys. He actually scored his only touchdown of the year on a great reception play that game. He had played his heart out that game, and when he could have easily let Bridgeport's extra point team send the game into overtime, he saw an open lane. He shot through the weakness in their offensive line and blocked the extra point with only seconds left to secure our win in a 49-48 "shoot-out". Ethan went on that season to be District MVP and First Team All State.

Kids Need Rules

We learned a lot about our team that night. Several of the boys found out they had a lot more stamina than they previously thought. Our boys dug deeper than they ever had before and we as a coaching staff saw some guys who deserved more playing time than they had previously gotten. We made a lot of changes after that to our offensive and defensive schemes.

The boys who sat learned a lot about themselves, too. The next week at practice, all seven guys at various times got up in front of the team and apologized. They told the team they had let them down and that it wouldn't ever happen again.

Some of them came to me personally later; a few of them in tears. They were afraid that I was going to think less of them because of the incident. I, of course, told them I didn't. They were good kids, and I knew that. That might make it harder for some people to have a more personal connection to their players, but we were relationally connected with all our boys. It didn't make any difference. When you make a rule, you have to stand by it. They need to see that kind of resolve.

Kids understand rules. They even want to be held to standards, though you'd never hear that from a 17 year-old. Even though we won the game, those 7 guys really felt the disappointment they cost the team. They learned a valuable lesson and got to see their coaches stand firm on a tough decision.

A few days later I found out that there was an over/under scheme in the bleachers that night. The start of the 4th quarter was the mark, and the bets were whether Coach McCoy would put the boys in before or after then to make sure he won the game.

A lot of people thought I was crazy for what I did. A lot of people thought I was going to throw away our perfect season just to make a point. I think Chance and Colt might have even thought that. But I knew it didn't make any difference. Our team needed to know that broken rules carry consequences. It brought the team together and we became stronger than we were before.

I was especially proud of my coaches that week for standing by me and supporting my decision. It was tough for them also as they listened to some of the criticism we were all getting. They were loyal and coached their tails off and were the real hero's that week.

I'd be lying if I said it wasn't tough to sit those boys. I was tempted to put them back in the game just like any coach would in my situation, but I'd already made up my mind days before so there really was no decision. When you know you have the right decision to make, you have to do it no matter how hard it is.

And, by the way, we didn't have any more issues the next 10 weeks of the football season. How often does that happen with high school boys?

We also went on to play for the 3A State Championship and had to beat Bridgeport again on our road through the playoffs.

Winning Well

Not every time you're forced to make a tough decision will you have ESPN there to catalogue it. Sometimes no one will ever know, and in a lot of ways, that's even harder. Who you see in the mirror has to be the person that others see as well.

Coaching football can be a tough row to hoe when it comes to integrity and character. On the one hand my heart is really into growing those boys to be men of greatness. On the other hand, no school ever paid me just because they were impressed with how many guys I could inspire to be better men. They also wanted wins on the scoreboard.

Balancing your passions (inspiring young men to be better men) and your job (motivating high school boys to score more points than other high school boys on Friday nights) is never easy. It's really nice when the two cross paths as much as mine did. There's a lot of people out there who think that to be a good coach, you've got to be really hard on the kids--that you really aren't the one in the position to make an impact on their lives other than making them better athletes. I disagree; I think you can make them better athletes who win more games and who learn how to win in life.

When coaching high school boys, it's a fore-drawn conclusion that 99% of them are not going to play in college, so my primary goal was always to make them into great men in any way I could. Football is a tremendous avenue to be able to teach that. But I also had to win, and the two really aren't mutually exclusive. If I was a softie on them because I didn't think winning was important and I only cared about their character, I'd be failing them just as much as if I viewed winning as the only thing in life.

Character and winning actually flow together in a perfect synergy, but no one joins a football team to learn character; they want to be winners. So you have to be intentional about building character. The hard work and discipline, telling your body to keep going when it wants to quit and the bangs and bruises from the violent sport of football are all beautiful life lessons. They just shouldn't be wasted in the name of winning games.

I was committed to building a winning team and boys who knew how to win at life, so I instituted some rules for our coaching staff. There's days where it really requires coming down pretty hard on a young man to get through his thick, teenage brain. Football is not the chess club—there's definitely yelling involved. And there are those times where that's what is required to push that young athlete on to the next level, but it's also the thing that can bruise a tender spirit.

If any of my coaches ever came down on a player during a practice or a game especially hard, they had to find that young man before he went home and give him a hug and affirm him. No slaps on the butt, no pats on the shoulder—it had to be a hug so that young man knew he was valued.

A hug may seem a little awkward for some people, but I believe its necessary for kids. I believed they needed to know that they were valued by us coaches as more than just tools to adding wins to our career. For a coach to take the effort to find that boy after practice and give him a hug goes a long way toward removing the embarrassment and wounds that are sometimes necessary to teach good football.

Winning is a part of life, but kids have to know it's important to win well. If we could teach these boys how to win with class and integrity then they could win in any area of their lives. We might have been building better linebackers and receivers then, but we were really building better CEO's and fathers for the future. So when we had to be a little rough with them it was important for us to follow that up with some words of affirmation.

The occasional tongue-lashing a boy gets in football isn't just a lesson for the field. There are definitely times where a boss has to have a difficult conversation with an employee and really set out some tough measures to get things done, but it doesn't have to be done with malice and belittling. That was the purpose of the hug. A tough lesson is much more easily learned when the lesson-giver is affirming.

I'm sure a lot of my coaches didn't want to have to give the boys a hug after practice if they'd been hard on them, but it was a non-negotiable. It was just too important for the kids' sake.

Letting Them Fail

It's pretty easy for parents and coaches to let their kids and athletes succeed on their own. It's fun to watch all your coaching and parenting pay off in a big success. What's hard is letting kids fail on their own.

It's so easy to step in and try to fix the problems a kid faces instead of letting them go through them alone with nothing more than a little supervision. When you see a science fair project that was obviously not put together by a 5th grader, you know where to look. We let parents get away with that all the time, but that's because I think we all sort of know what's going on. When their display looks like it was obviously put together by someone with a marketing degree it's not because that parent was just trying to give their kid an edge in the competition. More than likely what happened is the project wasn't going well and the parent just didn't want to see their kid fail. So they step in and get involved. And they get more involved. And still more involved. By the end they forget it was their kid's project in the first place.

Ever seen one of those before? I've been a teacher and a coach my entire career and I know that I certainly have.

We end up crippling our children and students when we as parents and coaches and teachers either take up the slack for them or make it too hard for those kids to fail. Every three year-old cries when he falls. But it's important for that little kid to learn what it feels like to get a little scuffed and bruised and then get back up. If we created environments where that child would never fall (good luck) we'd be stuck hearing the piercing whines and cries of twenty year-olds when they had their first spill. No thank you.

But it happens all the time when it comes to schoolwork, sports and other areas of life. It would have been a lot easier on me to cut Case some slack along the way when he was suffering from scleroderma, but I knew that as much as it made *my* life temporarily easier, it would make the rest of his life much more difficult.

That's why I felt like I had to hold our athletes to such high standards. When those boys in Graham came to me and were honest enough to confess their misdeeds, albeit minor, I was only tempted for a half-second to let them off the hook. I knew that they had to feel the pain of their choices. I just couldn't steal such a good lesson away from them.

But let's be honest; none of us hold that line perfectly. And when we don't, it's always bad for the kid and more often than not it comes back to bite us.

Working Harder

Being the football coach in small Texas towns comes with some great perks and some really hard decisions. The perks of the slow pace of life aren't for everyone, but the McCoys wouldn't really be at home anywhere else. The downside is that football coaches tend to have children who play football. Yeah, you see where this is going.

When your boy is on your team trying out for starting positions it would be really nice to recuse yourself from the decision, but it just doesn't work like that. I'm the coach, so I'm the one who has to make those decisions. And it just so happens that since my boys grew up around football they happened to be pretty good at it. It was bound to come naturally—they never missed a rock party from the time they were 3—football was in their blood.

What that makes difficult is not the assigning of starting positions, but doing it in a way where no parent or school administrator can accuse you of nepotism. I really had to "dot my i's and cross my t's" so to speak, when I was letting Colt, Chance and Case try out for the team. Everyone had to know that they earned their position just like everyone else.

What that equated to for my boys was that I was harder on them. Exceptionally harder. If they wanted to play quarterback on my team they didn't just have to be better than the other guys, they had to be measurably better. That's not to say there weren't other good quarterbacks when Colt and Case were on my team or great receivers when Chance was playing—there definitely were. But my boys knew I was going to make them perform well beyond anyone else to secure their spot. They knew that, and they worked very, very hard to get what they did.

I'm pretty sure I knew how to let my boys fail. I made them earn what they got on the football field and I let them own what they messed up. When they screwed up I'd come down on them harder than anyone else. That wasn't just to keep up appearances for parents, either. I wanted the other athletes to have the confidence to try out for positions knowing they weren't going to get snubbed just because the coach's son wanted to play quarterback. I also wanted my boys to know they really had to earn what they got.

When my boys were on my team it seemed much easier for me to let them fail. I knew they had the discipline and drive to get back up and keep trying without my intervention. But once they get out of the nest, it seems to get a litter easier to want to be protective. At least it did for me.

Your Daddy's Here

When Colt was in college playing for the Texas Longhorns he had a road trip to Lincoln to play the University of Nebraska Cornhuskers. Memorial stadium in Lincoln is one of the great American college football venues and I had already put a trip there on my "bucket list." We didn't get to make every one of Colt's away games, but I wasn't going to miss this one.

It's truly a great stadium and a great university with a wonderful football tradition. The fans at Nebraska are like almost nowhere else. That's to say, they're into the game, they're rowdy, and they're always ready to see Nebraska chew up and spit out the competition on their home turf. This time, though, the University of Texas and Colt McCoy were on the menu.

I had flown into Lincoln early that morning for a late afternoon start. It was a cold day in Nebraska with a beautiful light snow falling. I was at the stadium very early and decided to leave Debra in a local coffee shop and venture over to the field. I wanted to see the quarterbacks when they came out to start warm-ups. They always came out way before the other guys on the team.

As I made my way into the stadium I could hear lots of noise, but it was over two hours until kick-off and I couldn't figure out why there was such a commotion. When I walked up the walkway into the field I could see why. The stadium was virtually empty except for the three corner sections on the other side that were full of about 12,000 black-shirted, screaming Nebraska fans.

I started listening to the chants they were yelling and I could tell that they were directed at my son, who had taken the field for some warm-up throws. They were not exactly welcoming him to their home turf and I was kind of offended that they were treating him that way. I decided that I wouldn't let him take this abuse by himself. After all I was his coach *and* his dad—I could do something about this!

I walked down and around the stadium to the other side and came up on the field right next to where the Texas quarterbacks were warming up and right under the student section. I waved hello to Colt and had a brief handshake with Coach Davis (Texas' offensive coordinator) and stood with my chest poked out for being able to handle the abuse that was being chanted toward Colt.

In less than three minutes the whole student section was chanting, "Colt, your daddy's here! Colt, your daddy's here!" Colt was ticked off, waving for me to leave trying to get me off that field. Coach Davis was laughing pretty hard by that point and while I had come onto the field as the proud father that was helping his son, I left as a whipped pup with my tail between my legs.

All those years being extra hard on Colt and one game at a stadium that was unfriendly to him and I fell apart. The funny thing was that through the years I'd taught Colt to push out the naysayers and just focus on his game, and he was really good at it. He never even heard the jeers they were heckling him with until the deafening noise of their ridicule that his father was coming to defend him. I was so embarrassed.

We all want to protect our kids from harm, but there are just too many good lessons to learn along the way from suffering the consequences of their decisions or feeling a little pain of failure. It's just so important to hold the line with kids.

And if you're going to fail at holding that line, just try not to let your failures be in front of 12,000 screaming college kids.

Coach's Pep Talk

1. To lead the symphony, you must turn your back on the crowd.
2. Don't be a thermometer, be the thermostat.
3. The highest reward for a person's toil is not what they get for it, but what they become by it.

CHAPTER NINE

Notes On The Mirror

"**J**OY: Jesus, others, yourself."

Three sleepy-headed boys woke up to those powerful statements several mornings in a row. They were never uttered, only read. They appeared on the boys' bathroom mirror one day; the next iteration in a long list of messages scribbled across the steamy glass with an old tube of red lipstick.

There weren't many days that went by where there wasn't a note from Debra on the boys' mirror. She'd write something meaningful to them and leave it there for a few days until the condensation from the shower had made it almost illegible. Then it was time to wipe it off and write a new one.

It all started when the boys were old enough to go to school (and read, of course). She wanted to send little messages in their lunch boxes to let them know that she and their father loved them and thought about them. But they were *boys*. It didn't take long before Debra realized those were just going to be wasted words.

I mean, every boy does love his mother, but there's only so much cafeteria teasing a child can take about their "mommy writing them love notes" before they start finding their way to the first trash can in the school. It was a fight Debra knew she was going to lose one way or another and she wanted the boys to know day in and day out in an intentional way that their parents loved them. She wasn't going to give up.

She was rummaging through her bathroom drawer one morning and found an old tube of red lipstick that was almost empty but she'd never brought herself to throw away. That's when the epiphany came. If it was going to be too embarrassing in front of their friends, she could write to the boys where their friends would never see it. We've all heard of "lipstick on the mirror" and Debra thought, "why not?"

We don't remember what her first message was. She was just trying it out, so she didn't know then that it was going to become as routine to the McCoy household as milk and cereal in the mornings. I'm sure if we all had a premonition that something we did the first time was going to be a lasting tradition we'd probably take a lot more pictures of that inaugural event. We don't have a photo of that first lipstick message, but the idea stuck.

The boys didn't wipe it off, and that was the victory for Debra. I don't remember how things went at first--I'm sure the boys were a little grossed out by their mother writing them "love notes" on the mirror, but they quickly got used to them.

Sometimes the notes were scriptures. Sometimes they were Debra's version of Ben Franklin writing modern proverbs. Other times they were messages geared toward certain events, such as spelling bees and football games. The one thing they all had in common were that they were intentional words of love and affirmation from a loving mother.

Beyond Routine

Debra used the notes to reiterate the values and priorities we as a family talked often about. It was just one more way to tell the boys that we have to live life on purpose. But she didn't write the notes with any ideas of grandeur. She wrote them notes for years not thinking that she was having some nation-changing impact on the world, but just because it was one way a mother's heart could be expressed in a way three very *boyish* boys could understand it. The notes became such a part of the McCoy household that we almost never talked about them.

That's not to say they were just routine. Debra never let them go two weeks before the messages were changed out. She was intentional every day to see if the message needed to be changed. I wish now that we'd had a journal of them just to recall all the things Debra wrote to them over the years.

I'm a guy myself, so I have to admit that my routines meant that I didn't see every note she wrote to the boys. I guess I didn't have the patience a mother has to venture into the scary world of a bathroom that three boys share, especially during the teenage years. But I would peek in from time to time to see what she'd written. The messages would always make me smile.

Lifestyle

I know its not actually en vogue anymore, but having a mother at home full-time with children is really a wonderful blessing to a child's heart. When we started having children both Debra and I had already decided she was going to stay home from day one. We just didn't see the point in having someone else raise our kids when they didn't have to. How could they know the values we wanted to raise our kids with?

I don't want to be discouraging to the myriad of parents out there that raise their kids. This world is full of tough choices and difficult circumstances that people work hard to make the best of. Some people have to raise their children by themselves and others feel that both parents have to work outside the home. But we weren't fighting many of those battles. The choice for us was, were we willing to get by on just a poor rural Texas football coach's salary?

Since the answer was a definite yes that meant that we had to make lifestyle sacrifices. I don't want to say that we were poor, but beans and weenies were a staple at the McCoy house. We weren't poor, really, because we chose the lifestyle we were living. And we were happy to live it. That lifestyle is what gave us such a great home life with our boys.

The beans and weenies went away after I got promotions and better paying jobs, of course, but we never lived like kings. We lived within our means anywhere we went so that Debra could stay with the boys. And that afforded her some beautiful moments in the lives of three young men.

When Chance was born, Colt got the boot from his crib and had to start sleeping in a "big boy" bed. He was actually a little young for that, so Debra found that the whole bedtime routine was just a lot easier for us if she laid down with him every night until he fell asleep. She'd lay there with Colt reading bedtime stories or scripture to him and tell him how much she and his father loved him. I'd peek in many evenings to hear what was going on. It was always nice to know that we'd chosen a way of life that gave us such opportunities.

Consistency

The bedtime process was repeated for Chance and Case and as the boys got older the responsibility shifted to me. I'd go in at bedtime and pray with the boys before they went to sleep. We really believed in the power of a good night's sleep around our house, so we were pretty disciplined about bedtimes.

Kids really need that. They need the consistency of bedtimes and bed-time routines. Knowing that bedtime is fixed in stone (unless some sporting event kept them out later) and that Dad was going to spend a few minutes with them beforehand is comforting. It also makes parenting a lot easier.

It's interesting that you can chain an elephant to something sturdy when they're a baby and not strong enough to break away; they'll pull and tug on it, but eventually they learn it won't work and they resign themselves to their lot. Those same elephants as adults can be tied down with a flimsy rope to a little tent peg barely stuck in the ground and they'll never try to get away. They're certainly big enough to do *whatever* they please, but they never even try to pull on the rope. It's the same way with kids. If you establish routine disciplines over things like bedtimes early, and don't budge, it makes staying with those routines when they're older a lot easier.

But when you're tired and exhausted from a long day of work it can be difficult to fight those battles, even at a young age. That's what Debra staying home with the kids gave us—an adult in the house who hadn't spent all her energy during the day away from the kids. That's not to say in the least that what Debra did, staying home with three boys, was easy. But at the end of the day she knew she didn't have to get up early the next morning to face the work-routine again. It made our evenings so much easier.

Debra is my biggest hero. She gave up the satisfaction of work to raise our kids at an impressionable age. She kept our household running, and running well. She kept good food on the table and did it within our budget. Things were tight, but we never struggled and I owe that all to Debra's brilliance in running our house.

The boys didn't grow up watching a lot of television, either. They couldn't really. We always lived in little, out of the way places where cable didn't quite reach and long before DIRECTV. Our only options were a few staticky channels and kids videos, which we couldn't really afford at the time. So they spent a lot of time doing fun indoor activities and a *lot* of time outdoors.

Debra kept us eating on our meager budget in our early years and she kept the boys in clothes. She worked hard to keep a well-oiled machine running smoothly. We lived simply, but we were never poor because our boys had a mother who loved them and we had a roof over our heads. And it wasn't like Debra gave up a career forever. When Case, our youngest, started school, she went back to teaching.

Again, I don't want to discourage those out there that for one reason or another have to or choose to work and send their kids to daycare. But those out there who have a two-income family just to keep your house stocked with stuff, is it really worth it? We decided early on that it wasn't, and we've never regretted it. We've never regretted the nice television we didn't have—that by now certainly would be in the land-fill anyway. We never regretted the nice meals at restaurants we didn't get to eat—we never had that many close to our house anyway. What we really never regretted, though, was wondering what it would have been like to watch our little sons grow up.

Living Life On Purpose

Debra and I had the privilege to see three baby boys grow up into men while we were really paying attention. It may not be an option for every-one, but if it can be, why wouldn't you take it? There's always more stuff to buy, but there's not always a four-year old boy around asking for your attention.

I'm telling you what we did and what our home life looked like. I cer-tainly don't think it was the model home; I'm pretty sure that doesn't exist. But it was a life we chose on purpose. We were intentional about how we lived and I believe we lived better for it. The way our home worked may not be the way yours can or should look, but however your home looks, make sure it's because you chose for it to be that way.

Don't let the days turn into months and years without telling your children how you feel about them. Don't let the opportunities to teach and train them with life's values pass you by. Lipstick is cheap, but when it's written on a child's bathroom mirror into words of love and affirmation it becomes priceless. We know that they never wondered if we loved them or not.

Good Influences

I decided when we started having kids that I was going to be those boys' best friend. That's not to say I wasn't going to be their father, too. I wasn't going to slack up on discipline and punishment when the boys needed it, but I was going to let them know that I was there for them all the time. Some people think you can only have it one way or the other. I don't believe so.

At the end of my coaching career, I went to work in the Sports Division of the Flippen Group—an executive development and organizational consulting company. I have known the president, Flip Flippen, for many years. He loves to say, "If you don't have a child's heart, you have no business messing with his head." Long before I heard that poignant phrase, it was how I wanted our family to run. I always wanted my boys to understand that I loved them and there were reasons I had to punish them or tell them no. I told them there were going to be times they weren't going to like me very much, but that they were definitely going to know that I love them.

Even though I wanted to be the boys' best friend *and* father, both Debra and I knew we couldn't do it all. We knew the boys were going to find other people to mentor them, whether they thought of it like that or not. All too often kids make bad decisions about whom they let be that voice, so we decided we were going to find people for them.

Everywhere we lived we were always on the lookout for older boys in our churches and schools who could be a good influence on our boys. We wanted them to see young men who were developing good character and setting good priorities so they could learn from them.

It's so easy for kids to go wrong when they pick the wrong friends. Just think about how many good people you know whose kids have gone down the wrong path. Many times it's just that they fell into the wrong crowd. When Debra and I found older boys we thought were of good character, we were trying to cut those bad decisions off at the pass, if you will. We hoped to teach Colt, Chance and Case how to choose good friends. If we didn't teach them, how were they going to know what good influences look like?

I don't want it to sound like we chose all our boys' friends for them—we didn't. But we tried very hard to steer them in the right direction so that they knew how to make good choices in friends. No kids are perfect, but we can spare our children from so many bad decisions by simply knowing who they spend their time with.

When The Lipstick Was Found

We rarely ever let our boys sleep over at other boy's houses. We just didn't know what the environment was going to look like for them, unless they were close family friends, and if we couldn't be sure how it was going to look the answer was always "no." Our boys didn't like that so much at first, but as they grew older they began to realize our reasoning for it. There's a lot of trouble that kids can get into when the other kids' parents aren't around or paying attention.

We did let them have other boys over to our house for sleepovers once in a while, and we loved it. It was always interesting to see everyone's reaction to the lipstick messages on the boys' mirror. Sometimes our boys were a little embarrassed. The older they got, the more they were used to it and it was just something our family did. Our boys knew that not every one of their friends had parents who went out of their way to let them know they cared and thought about them, and I know it meant more to them as they grew older (although I know it never meant as much to them as it did to Debra and I).

Debra never put the lipstick on the mirror for anyone else to find, but it was always funny when another boy did. Sometimes there was a little teasing, other times the boy would get a pensive look like he was thinking about the things his parents did like that for him.

I know that there's lots of other great ways that parents show their love to their children. Most of the boys that did come over felt that love from their parents, but they'd never seen anything like Debra's lipstick messages. It may have been a quirky McCoy thing, but it was one more thing that made our family who it was.

And Debra never ran out of great things to say.

Attention Wal-Mart Shoppers

We were a very traditional Christmas family. Spending the eve and waking up at grandparents' house with all the cousins and seeing what Santa had brought the night before. We would watch *White Christmas* and *It's a Wonderful Life* every Christmas Eve whether we wanted to or not. That was just the way we did it. But when the boys were in early elementary school we wanted to have a Christmas celebration within our own small family.

Debra had so many good ideas with the boys through the years. She was always so creative at making our budget stretch as far as it could. Christmas was one of those times for us, like many families, where the budget needed some serious stretching. She came up with a great idea one year, and much to our surprise, Wal-Mart security hasn't ever picked us up.

I'm sure they must have thought about it. I mean, here's this family of five who come tearing through the front doors looking like five cats about to eat a canary. Then they split up into two groups, grab two shopping carts, and head off in two different directions. Wearing oversized winter coats, they run up and down the aisles, whispering and giggling, grabbing stuff off of shelves, and trying to cover all the merchandise with their coats.

It must have looked really suspicious. But we really weren't doing anything wrong. We were just taking part in what would eventually become an official Brad-and-Debra-McCoy family tradition.

Debra had the idea to take the boys to Wal-Mart and let them buy Christmas presents for each other (nothing expensive, I think we had something like a $10 limit for each gift).

While we always had a good time, the first few years we did this were a little challenging.

Anyone who's ever had kids knows when they're really little, it's pretty much "all about me." It takes a while for kids to get hold of the "you" part. I mean, even for a grownup, it's not an easy thing to try and figure out what somebody else might like as a gift. I know I still struggle with it (just ask Debra!).

So the first few times we did the Wal-Mart thing, Debra and I had to give the boys a lot of guidance, like, "You know guys, I'm not sure Mom is all that crazy about Power Rangers." But they eventually caught on and even got really good at it!

Debra would take one or two of the boys and I would take the other one or two, and we'd head off with our shopping carts to opposite ends of the store. Whoever Debra was shopping with would look for gifts for me and whoever was with me, and vice versa. Then we would meet up in the middle of the store, exchange children and do it all over again.

The gifts were supposed to be a surprise. The object of the game was to get out of the store without anybody knowing what they were getting. Of course, since somebody had to pay for them, Debra and I always knew what they'd picked out. But it took them a few years to figure that out.

The whole thing was kind of like a big "undercover" game for the boys. We would pick out gifts and then the boys would spend the rest of the time trying to keep everything covered up so that the other "team" couldn't see what was in the basket.

As soon as we got home, everybody would take the gifts they had picked out, run to their rooms, and quickly wrap them. And I thought Wal-Mart was challenging! That was nothing compared to three young boys with scissors, paper, and tape, all chomping at the bit to open some presents.

After all the gifts were wrapped, the boys brought them into the living room. We passed them out and they would open them one at a time— the giver was always so proud. It was a blast.

Lipstick Fades

Presents and toys aren't what make a great Christmas. Colt, Chance and Case had fun because we made it fun (but the presents and toys helped— at least in their minds). And they knew they had parents who loved them and they loved each other like brothers do.

Our family probably doesn't look like yours and it really doesn't need to. I'm not saying it should, I only wanted to share that the McCoys weren't all football helmets and sweaty jerseys. And we owe that almost entirely to Debra. She is a phenomenal woman who demonstrated excellence in a house full of testosterone. The fact that she stayed home with our boys during their most formative years makes me fall in love with her all over again time after time.

Debra never took her job raising our boys at home lightly. The lipstick on the mirror wasn't the only thing she did. She was constantly trying to find ways to teach those boys and tell them we loved them. It was Debra who held the line with the boys most of the time. She had more than one discussion about "how many adults are going to be at this party?" It was she who made sure everyone was where they needed to be when they needed to be there. I'll forever be her biggest fan.

But there are no more Christmas Wal-Mart trips these days and the lipstick on the mirror is rare now that the boys are all gone. We're "empty-nesters" with only memories of those days now, but that doesn't stop us from continuing to show our love to the kids. There's never a week that goes by where the boys don't at least get a text from Debra or I reminding them to do their best and be a leader.

And there *certainly* aren't too many days that go by that their mother doesn't hear from them.

At least there'd better not be!

Coach's Pep Talk
1. He that dies with the most toys dies anyway.
2. The gap between more and enough never closes.
3. Yesterday is history, tomorrow is a mystery but today is a gift.

CHAPTER TEN

The Second Half

It was like everything just stopped. The fans stopped. The band stopped. The players stopped. There must have been seven or eight thousand people there that night and they all just *stopped*.

There's an unspoken rule in football that coaches and players stay on their own sidelines during a game. In fact, there's a box outlined on each sideline for the team to stand within. But we had just broken that rule.

It was almost the end of the 4th quarter and the Wylie Bulldogs had just scored a late touchdown against my team, the Graham Steers, that put the game out of reach. There were still a few minutes left to play in this intense rivalry when I signaled the referee for a timeout.

I started across the field accompanied by Cody, one of my senior captains. I'm sure everybody thought we were either crazy or about to start a fight, or maybe both. I mean, it's not really something you see every day—a coach and a player wandering across the field in the middle of a football game.

I think we really confused the referees, who had been making their way toward us when they saw what we were doing. They started shouting and waving their arms in the air, and I couldn't hear what they were saying but I figured it wasn't good.

I stopped at midfield, raised my hand, and waved them off. I knew they wanted us off the field, but they weren't making a big deal of it. They just sort of stepped back and watched.

Cody and I talked for a few seconds and then he turned and continued across the field towards the opponent's sideline by himself while I stood and waited.

The First Step

You could have heard a pin drop when Cody's blue and red jersey disappeared into a sea of purple and gold Bulldog jerseys.

After several minutes, Cody emerged from the Bulldogs' sideline and walked back across to midfield. I gave him a high-five, and then we turned and jogged back to our own sideline.

The sound of faint clapping coming from the Wylie side broke the silence. By the time we got back to our sidelines, that faint clapping had erupted into thunderous applause. Cody and I looked up to see the entire stadium on their feet, cheering and shouting.

They were cheering and shouting for Cody—the young man who was willing to take the first step.

The last several years, the rivalry between Wylie and Graham had been getting ugly. Players were taking cheap shots—late hits, unnecessary roughness, etc. There was definitely some bad blood between these two teams.

While some Wylie players had taken cheap shots on some of my players the previous year, it was my team dishing them out this year.

It had been a really tough game. My players were tired and frustrated, but they were still fighting hard. Then Wylie scored that touchdown. The Wylie fans were already on their feet celebrating when the kicker set up for the extra point.

Cody tried to block the kick, but was too late. The ball was already in the air. The second he saw the ball leave the kicker's foot he should have stopped. But he didn't. He ran right through him. It was a flagrant foul—as plain as day.

When Cody hit the kicker, I looked across the football field at Coach Sandifer, the head coach at Wylie. We had been good friends for a long time and he is a great coach. He was standing there with both arms out to the sides, palms up, and his shoulders shrugged up all the way to his ears.

I didn't have to hear the words to know what he was trying to say. It was the exact same gesture I had made to him from across the field the year before.

It meant, "What's the deal?"

There was no doubt Cody had wronged the Bulldog kicker. Although, to this day I still don't think Cody was trying to hurt anyone. He was a good kid. It was just one of those situations where restraint was called for, but fatigue, frustration, and disappointment got the better of him.

But that didn't make it right. It shouldn't have happened. I knew it. He knew it. Coach Sandifer knew it. And when the celebratory sounds coming from the Wylie side turned to booing and hissing, it was obvious they knew it too.

I suppose if it had been any other night, we might have just taken the penalty and let it go. After all, it *was* football. This kind of stuff happened all the time. And nobody got hurt. It was just "part of the game," right?

That's the first thing that came to mind. Then I remembered the saying I always used with my coaches:

> *If something goes wrong on the field, you're either coaching it or accepting it.*

And something had definitely gone wrong. Since I knew I hadn't coached my team to commit personal fouls, I had to make a decision in that moment whether or not I was going to accept those fouls—if I was going to live up to my mantra.

So I pulled my headset off and met Cody as he was coming off the field and said, "I'd like us to walk across the field, find the kicker, and tell him that's not the way we play football in Graham."

I don't think he believed me at first. His mouth fell open and his eyes got as wide as saucers, like, "Really, Coach? Are you serious? We're going to do that?"

I explained to him that I wasn't trying to embarrass him—this really wasn't about him. It was about doing the right thing; about making amends for doing the wrong thing; about being willing to be the first to say you were wrong; about honoring the game we loved after it had been dishonored.

When the two of us were standing there in the middle of the field, I asked Cody if he wanted to go on by himself or if he wanted me to go with him. I wanted him to understand that I was totally prepared to go all the way with him if he needed me to, but that it was something he really needed to do on his own.

He never once hesitated. He knew immediately what he had to do. He gave me a nod, turned, and walked on—alone.

He had to roam around on the Bulldog's sidelines for a few seconds to find the kicker—after all, he was looking for a number, not a face. When he finally found him, Cody reached out, shook his hand, and apologized. Then he walked over to the Wylie coach and did the same.

When Cody got back to midfield, I told him, "I'm proud of you, son."

It's so easy when we're tired, frustrated and defeated to just give up. That's when we need to realign ourselves with our priorities the most. If I'd let Cody (and even worse, myself) get away with what happened, we would have suffered more than a devastating loss that night. We would have suffered a demoralizing blow to our team's identity. We dealt with a problem that night, and while we didn't win the game, we came out winners in the end in much more important ways.

We have to always remember that until our game's over, there's always time to make things right.

The Second Half

The thunder of the crowd noise above us still thundered. The rhythmic sounds of cheering and stomping had put Colt into something of a trance for a moment. Then the team trainers asked Colt to put on his street clothes back on and go back onto the field. That woke him up.

"No way!" Colt told them. "I'm going back out there suited up." He immediately threw his pads and jersey back on and went looking for his helmet. He wasn't going back on the field in street clothes to let his team know that he'd given up. He was going back to the field fully engaged in the battle they were in.

The helmet was hard to find, though. The trainers had wisely hidden it earlier because they knew Colt's competitive spirit and what this game meant to him. They had locked his helmet up in a trunk to prevent anything Colt might have decided to do on his own. He would have done anything to get back in the game.

He finally gave up looking for his helmet and went back onto the sidelines with his pads on. He quickly grabbed a headset and got involved in the offensive scheme so he could help backup quarterback Garret Gilbert in any way he could.

I went back to my seat and watched something remarkable at the Rose Bowl that night. I watched as my son lost the greatest opportunity on the grandest stage of his life. He'd dreamed of this moment all his years and worked tirelessly to get there. He'd sacrificed so many things through the years just to be here and now it was gone. In a moment all he'd worked for was gone.

And he never quit.

I looked on with great pride as my son went from being a player to a coach. He listened to every play the offensive coordinator called. He counseled the freshmen Gilbert on strategies to pick apart the Alabama defense he'd studied so tirelessly. As I watched him lean into Gilbert's ear and shout to be heard over the crowd noise I imagined he was telling him which linebacker to watch for when he began inching forward for a blitz. I could see in his eyes, from halfway across the stadium, his mind running a hundred miles an hour thinking of ways he could give his team the advantage he felt they had started with.

And they came very close. Garrett Gilbert led a valiant effort and came just within reach in the second half of taking the game back, but the deficit of the first half proved to be just too much.

As time expired I sat there with my wife just speechless. By that moment my mind was almost a complete blank. It's hard to describe the emotions that go on inside of you after an event like that. You don't know how any day will end when you start it, but we never could have imagined how *that* day would end.

We sat in the stadium for a long time until almost everyone else had left. We sat there and soaked in the sights and sounds and let the whole drama just sink in. Debra and I just sat, phones buzzing continually, and remembered our son's dream of making it to this level. I thought about how he'd done it with discipline, character and perseverance. I thought about how he didn't deserve for this to happen to him. I wondered why it had happened to him.

I often think about someone who has lost a child or a loved one tragically. It makes me sick to think about their loss and how my experience was over a game. I speak apologetically when I tell this story because the pain and grief that Debra and I felt that day, and still do, is so small in comparison to what so many people have walked through.

But the hurt is real. I think about what it would be like to look into my boy's eyes and see that glimmer from the guy who'd won the college football national championship. I think about how I would feel to see that championship ring on my son's finger. And I think about how he'll never get another shot at it. There's too many "what-if's" to list and every one of them causes me pain. They all turn my stomach because five plays into the biggest game of my son's life he had it all taken away.

And we'll probably never get any answers as to why things happened the way they did. My pain when I think about it may never go away, but my pride swells when I think about how my son rose to the occasion in the second half. He never gave up. He never said, "I'm done." When his opportunity was taken away he determined he was going to help everyone else achieve it instead.

We were sitting in the stadium through the celebration and the postgame wrap up in our mixture of stunned silence and parental pride so we knew nothing of what was going on down on the field. Not long after the game I started getting texts and messages from *everyone* I knew about how touched they were by Colt's words after the game. I didn't know what he said to the cameras, but I knew it must have been good.

We made our way through the traffic jam after the game that seemed like an eternity of cars to someone from Graham, Texas and arrived back at the team hotel after midnight. I went into Colt's room and found him sitting on the bed silently reflecting on the evening. I went in and gave him a hug and told him how proud of him I was.

But I had to know, "What did you say on camera after the game, Colt?"

"I'm not really sure, Dad," was his puzzled reply.

"Well, whatever you said, it must have been good," I told him. "Really, what did you say, son?"

"Dad, I'm really not sure of my exact words. I wasn't prepared for the questions they were going to ask me. I just hope I gave a good answer," Colt said.

I stayed up until 2 am or so watching Sports Center before they showed the replay of his post-game interview. When I heard his words, I was overcome with pride and joy. I felt like *I* may just as well have won the Super Bowl. The reality that my son could speak with such faith and poise in the midst of what I knew was absolutely the most difficult thing he'd ever gone through made me the happiest father in the world that night.

I mean, there was Colt, walking off the field after what was unquestionably the biggest disappointment of his football career. And as Colt was making his way to the locker room through the melee of people swarming the field a camera crew and reporter stopped him to ask him the question that we were all asking, "How are you feeling after such a big disappointment and loss?" Colt's response was amazing.

> *"I always give God the glory. I never question why things happen the way they do. God is in control of my life and I know that if nothing else, I'm standing on the rock,"*

That statement would come back time and time again over the next several months as I travelled and spoke for the Flippen Group. I've met so many people who told me Colt's words that evening changed their lives.

Mind, Body, Spirit

That night was like a whirlwind for months afterward. Debra and I would just stare puzzled at each other for weeks as if to say, "did all that really happen?" There are so many painful and joyful emotions wrapped up in that event for me. On the one hand, I watched as my son had a pretty decent chance to win a national championship disappear in one play.

On the other hand, I watched him become more of who he'll be the rest of his life.

When Colt came back out during the second half he was doing something far greater than winning a national championship; he was helping to give someone else the opportunity to do so. He fought hard for his team that night in every way he could and in the end they came up short. The Alabama Crimson Tide won the national championship, and they deserve great credit for playing well.

In the end, though, football's just a good means to a better end. Will Colt be the first 60-year old to play in the NFL? Not a chance! No matter how good an athlete you are, you can never compete at the top level forever. We can work hard and push our bodies far beyond what we might have ever imagined they were capable of, but there's only so far and so long we can push them. Our mind, will and spirit, however—there's no end to how far we can push them.

We preached to our boys to fill their bodies with the right fuel to keep them running right just like you would a car to keep it running smoothly. Whereas that's still great advice even if you're 95, if you don't fill your mind with the proper fuel along the way what you put in your body won't be of much use.

Through all my years as a coach I was always interested in seeing my athletes grow up to be great men—good husbands, honest businessmen and great leaders. Most of them would never play college ball, but even for those who went all the way to the pros, football eventually comes to an end. How they live the rest of their lives was far more important. I committed to myself to teach every boy that played on my team how to succeed in life.

Will I be intentional?

Will I refuse to lower my standards?

Will I set good priorities for my life and my family?

Will I persevere through tough times and never let excuses keep me from my goals?

Will I make the tough decisions even if no one is watching?

Will I leave a legacy?

These are the questions I wanted every one of my student athletes asking throughout their lives.

Home Field Advantage

The home field advantage on the football field is a powerful ally. There's nothing scientific about it—I'm sure there have been studies done and things like that—but it's just something intangible. Maybe it's the fact that it's your own turf. Maybe it's the fact that the fans are cheering for you. Or maybe it's the fact that you know exactly where every bump in your own field is. You can't say exactly what it is, but playing at home just seems to give you an edge.

There's so many times in life we don't feel like we're "playing at home." The McCoy family certainly didn't feel like we were romping around our back yard when we were watching our littlest one go through painful testing over and over again, not knowing what Case's outcome would be. We were never quite at home during the loss of Debra's parents—in a span of eight years the boys lost one set of grandparents. We were never quite at home when the boys lost their cousin, Grant, who had fought through two tours in Iraq. We were never quite at home with the multiple moves we made. Colt certainly wasn't at home in a stadium in California full of fans cheering on a team without him.

But in life, the home field advantage isn't about where you are. It's about who you are. It's about what values and priorities you take with you. The McCoy clan really was playing on our home field every time we went with Case to Scottish Rite hospital in Dallas. We had each other and we were going to stick together no matter what. And we were never going to quit, no matter how bad it may have gotten for Case. Even when Case told Colt and Chance they could stay home, they'd refuse. The affirmation and devotion of brothers was better than thousands of cheering fans.

We really were on our own turf during move after move after move. As a family we pressed through the difficulties of saying good-bye and we each looked forward to making new friends. We all decided to "do our best and be leaders" everywhere we went. That statement was the "stadium lighting" that illuminated every little bump in our home field. Having that phrase in our back pocket saved us all from so many bad decisions through the years (you didn't think that just because we *said* it to our boys every day it wasn't stuck in Debra and my heads too, did you?).

What's your home field? Do you have the things necessary to take your home field into any situation you encounter?

We take that home field with us every time we're intentional about the things we do with our family or team or company. When we purpose ourselves to do things on purpose with a purpose we overcome so many obstacles that often hold us down.

We take our home field advantage with us when we keep that bar high with the people around us and with ourselves. When we refuse to lower our standards we take away the crippling effects of so many bad decisions that result from our choices without proper guides.

We carry our home field with us all the times we make our priorities clear and simple. When you don't have to navigate a mountain of confusing and sometimes conflicting priorities our decisions become so much clearer and easier.

Our home field comes along with us when we refuse to make excuses for our shortcomings. When we take away the options of excuses, we have no other option but to face the reality of our situation and how much of it we've caused. When we do that, we can more easily correct the things that have gone wrong and turn our situation around.

Home field advantage looks like establishing activities and events in our lives that create great traditions. When we build into our lifestyles traditions that foster our priorities and values we make indelible markers that remind us of where we're heading and where we've been.

Perseverance brings the home field advantage along with us. Refusing to accept defeat and pressing on through difficult circumstances gives us the resolve and fortitude to overcome besetting challenges and achieve our goals. There's no goal that can't be achieved through perseverance.

We're on our home field when we make the tough decisions no matter the consequences. When we refuse to cower to the whims of others or even ourselves when we feel like shrinking back we push ourselves onward toward greatness.

And our home field is ours when we remember the softer side of life. We have to take time to remember the important people in our lives and how they make us better and spur us on toward greatness. No one has any success in life alone—we need the people in our lives that leave us those "notes on the mirror."

No, you can't take thousands of cheering fans, a field full of freshly cut grass or bright stadium lights with you everywhere you go. Your locker room doesn't travel along with you through life, and it's always tiring to travel outside your comfort zone. But you never have to leave the benefits of your home field at home.

The home field is wherever you make it—wherever you take your priorities and live out your goals on purpose. That's a lot easier said than done, though. I should know. I haven't always lived up to my goals. I haven't always been very good about being intentional, and I've failed miserably too many times to count when it comes to making excuses. There's no aspect of this book that I can't claim failures in on multiple levels, but that's never been a valid excuse for me.

Even though I've failed many times, I'll never give up trying to live out my values. I'll never forget my priorities in life. I won't give up on my goals. I may have blown the "first half" of my game in so many ways, but just like football, in life we always have a "second half" to do better.

Maybe you feel like you haven't done so well with your first half, but there's still another half to go. As long as there's still time on the clock, there is always HOPE (Romans 5:3-5).

And the home field advantage is always yours.

Contact the Author

To schedule Brad McCoy for an event or interview, or for more information on Flippen Group products and services, call, email or visit us online.

call: 1-888-608-8488

email: chad.chmelar@flippengroup.com

web: www.flippengroup.com

@coachbradmccoy

facebook.com/flippengroup

You can order additional copies of Home Field Advantage today at flippensports.com/homefield

The Flip Side
Breaking Free of the Behaviors That Hold You Back

A New York Times Best Seller
By Flip Flippen

Do you ever wonder why your life isn't going where you want?

Do you feel like no matter how hard you work, you can't accomplish what you want?

Do you wonder why others are more successful in relationships than you are?

Leadership expert and executive coach Flip Flippen will show you how your personal constraints affect your life... and how you can conquer them! "Flip" your negative attitudes into positive action with The FLIP SIDE, a proven life-changing new approach to overcoming the constraints that are holding you back in every area of your life.

Available at flippensports.com/homefield

10690020R0

Made in the USA
Lexington, KY
13 August 2011